The Secret War

The Secret War

The Heavens Speak Of The Battle

Heidi Hollis

Writers Club Press

San Jose New York Lincoln Shanghai

Writers Club Press
an imprint of iUniverse.com, Inc.

For information address:
iUniverse.com, Inc.
5220 S 16th, Ste. 200
Lincoln, NE 68512
www.iuniverse.com

ISBN: 0-595-20331-0

Printed in the United States of America

This book is dedicated to all those who have fought in this war and gave their lives for others that were not even aware of their sacrifice.

I would also like to thank these and other unseen heroes for their support, enlightenment and encouragement to keep strong in this effort to bring this story forward in hopes of helping others against so many odds.

Dear Aliens,

You have come,
and said I was the one.

You said, I agreed,
Yet you came to me with greed.

You, are the Grays,
but then other ones came my way.

They brought me love, light and joy,
and warned me that you were the ones to avoid.

Now you cannot even come near me,
besides, you never could, really.

All I had to do was listen,
so all that comes my way, now glistens.

Sincerely,
Heidi

CONTENTS

FOREWORD

Herein lies my heart and soul. Putting this book together has not been an easy task, but its been the only one on my mind for the past four years.

I got the inclination to begin to write this book while I was a full-time student, achieving my Bachelor of Science degree in Occupational Therapy. I had two years left of school and internships, when suddenly I was faced with what my true goals were to be in life.

Almost sadly school was not a part of it, not once I recalled my true purpose. Upon learning this purpose all I could think of was dropping everything to pursue my calling. Nothing else seemed to matter to me, but to follow my heart and what it had reminded me of.

Had I not received the encouragement from a physically distant yet so very close friend, I would have not finished school. My friend told me that it was necessary for me to continue on to finish my degree, so that I may tell my story and have that piece of paper that spelled "credibility" to some people. That somehow, that degree would help prove to people that those involved with the UFO and alien phenomena were sane and intelligent people like everyone else.

I knew my friend was right, and I continued on in school, struggling to keep my mind focused on attaining this supposed credibility. Now, I have it and now I'm speaking.

Personally I don't feel any more credible than I did before. But for what it's worth, a career in things other than the paranormal does await me now to tap into when the time comes. But for now I've chosen not to pursue my studied career because there are some things that are more important than prestige or money.

I've been needing to share some things, that I hope can and will help people open up to a new possibility as to how our world works. I only say "possibility," because many will think of what I'm saying here to be only an opinion. For me, I know what's expressed in here to be true. But my goal is not to convince anyone of anything that's said in these pages. It's not my place to do so.

In here, I'm going to detail a part of my life that unexpectedly led into defining the lives of us all that reside on this planet. There's so much to be said, to paint a full picture of everything would not be possible. So I only offer to lift the curtain a bit in revealing what's at hand. I understand that much of what needs to be said here will seem too profound to take to heart for some people.

But I do hope people take note that I, like many other people involved in UFO and other paranormal phenomena, are your neighbors, your sisters, your brothers, your police officers, your doctors, or even your own parents. I am like everyone else, but you might not know what comes to me at home in the middle of the night or broad daylight. These topics are not the easiest to speak to your everyday person about, so often times they are kept hidden.

No one likes to be looked at as being different or out of the norm, so we often keep up on the latest styles and trends so as not to stick out of a crowd. So imagine if it were yourself that found themselves in knowledge of a reality that was all around everyone, but unknown to most. You might feel isolated, or that you were losing your grip on things, or you might just be the type of person to trudge up the courage to speak out about what you've learned and seen.

Then imagine turning to the person standing next to you listening to you speak about your experiences that most don't acknowledge to happen but in the movies. You might be met with a smirk, laughter or even Biblical quotes that give all the credit for any alien contact or paranormal knowledge you may have to the devil and his crafty work.

This isn't the route to choose if you are looking to live in harmony with societal norms. Nor is speaking on the paranormal a way to make a quick buck.

So I just hope those that read this material, take into account the full spectrum of what goes into taking a step forward to speak up, no matter what others may think. For myself it's a passion so deep and burning, it was not even an option to keep silent just because what others may think.

I know what's written here may challenge a lot of what people believe in, but I know most of it will fall within what's already been discussed for centuries. My language can be quite frank, modern and even humourous whenever I write or speak on this topic, to me it's the most human and relative way I find to communicate. But none of what I say, I do to insult or belittle. If someone finds something not savvy to their tune, by all means take what you want out of it at your discretion. I can only hope most people will come away with some small piece of information that will help them through the times ahead that are duly noted as *the end times*.

I only ask, nothing.

A Short Story: *Alien Perspective at a Glance*

Imagine it, space, deep, dark and wondrous. You're a traveler venturing out, coming from a distant place of different meaning. You pass several planets in many galaxies with lots of different life forms that are very much aware of your presence and technology.

You move on.

You continue to meet and sometimes greet those you come into contact with, then you come across a particular part of the galaxy that is out of tune from what you are used to. You see a brightly lit star with various sized planets rotating around it. These planets look mostly barren and bleak with nothing to offer, to explore or learn about.

They are merely gray and brown, with no tolerable atmosphere to speak of. There's no life, no one to exchange knowledge with or to speak with. You then put your transportation into high gear to trudge onward in hopes of passing this ghastly sight as quickly as you can.

As you near closer to this emanating star, you unexpectedly see a marvelous glow coming into view.

You count, "One, two, three planets from the star."

There's a pulsating blue hue coming from this third planet in sight. It surely stands out from the rest, you can clearly see an atmosphere extending clear beyond the edges of this planet. There is also a mixture of pure white clouds, swirling in the midst and green, permanent masses on the surface. It's alive!

"No doubt there are beings that live here then," you think to yourself. "But where are they? Why are they not here to hail and ask of my presence here?"

You lower down for a closer look and find the inhabitants cannot see you with their technology. You come down even closer then, you can now see the richness of this planet, the foliage, the water and the very life force of the planet itself.

You settle your transportation down on the ground and exit your vehicle. You begin to walk among some of the inhabitants and find some can see you, while others cannot. Some respond to you in fear, while others regard you as a god.

You soon learn from them, that these beings only know the restrictions of their physical bodies and stay within those means. They value power, rank and are very materialistic, and yet very primitive in comparison to what you have access to. There is nothing here to learn from in a technical sense, but they are unique in their being.

There is laughter, pain and emotion, some things that you are not as familiar in having to deal with personally. You are astonished at how these few things rule the society of the beings that are here. Then you are introduced to the ones that claim to be in charge of the others there.

They marvel at your technology and the very difference of the make up of your body. They seek to have some of these technologies you possess so that they may learn how to quiet their neighbors that threaten them with war due to their petty differences. You look into their eyes and through your abilities, you can see that they wish to be superior at all costs. That nothing matters to these beings, not the planet's well-being and not each other.

You can also see that their very souls have been neglected and that these beings hardly regard it's existence. These beings need to be taught more than technology, but selflessness and respect for one another.

What do you do?

There's so much potential to go one way or the other to use this contact to your, or their advantage. You call upon your roots, where you come from and your values on how to proceed. What you may decide could lay the foundations forever in the relationship between these beings and those of your kind that come along next.

So what values or whom do you represent to make this historical decision?

1

REASONINGS: *THE BASICS*

Everyone has a soul. But what of animals, plants, and bacteria, can they also be considered into that group as having souls? They all respond to their environment, most experience pain or discomfort, and have goals to accomplish in their daily lives. So why not include them in that category as having souls?

Easily one can make the distinction that if these various life forms have souls, they are indeed different from human souls, that's a given. But still their existence of *being* is a fact, and that's true whether or not you believe they are something more than the shell they move about in. Most people who have ever had a pet in their lives, would most likely stress that there is something more to their pet than just fur.

If that can be settled, there should be little problem in accepting the fact that extraterrestrial beings also have a soul. First of course, one would have to acknowledge that life does exist outside of our little realm of reality here on Earth. Then that may also mean that if they have souls, theirs are somewhat different from human souls. Different, but not as human's are to animals.

For people that sometimes have a hard time understanding how life could exist elsewhere and take more comfort in the word of scientists instead of the person next to them, I offer this piece of information:

*If microscopic organisms can be found in a chunk of rock that fell from Mars, and it takes smaller organisms to make bigger ones, well then I feel pretty confident that there are bigger ones out there.

Our own bodies are a testament that we are dependent on smaller organisms to survive, such as the mitochondria which are literally the power house of the cells in the human body. Without the symbiotic relationship we have with other organisms, we just wouldn't be the same. Then we have scientists discovering micro-organisms from elsewhere, and are so impressed by this and other things, that they have several projects now scouring our galaxies for other life forms or even mere traces of water.

I feel confident that our government's of this world would not put so much into so many projects, publicly even, if there was nothing to be had. The imagination can take you far, but to have matters of evidence, that can take you even farther and inspire you even more. The proof of extraterrestrial life is everywhere if you truly look at all the angles from cave wall paintings, to the scribbling's of a three year old child's of visitors in the night.

Needless to say, I'm a believer of there being other life out there, even if I never had seen and known aliens for myself. Just as a note, I'll use the term "alien," only because it is easier for others to identify what that means (and I don't have some earthy, holistic term for them either). But if I just so happen to know the alien personally, I like to call them by their name.

Yes they have names and they have souls too and yes I do know some, and they happen to have a story to tell. In fact I would not be writing this book if it were not for their urgent pleadings. All I know is that this must be done and told, so you know. So everyone knows what is going on right on your own world, right before your closed eyes.

First I should take this all from the beginning.

I'd like to give a little background on where I am coming from and how I came to knowing what is on some of the alien's minds. I realize it's important to have a foundation to see where a person has been and it makes it easier to note how they've arrived to where they are now.

I have been looking into this whole UFO thing for over 15 years now, mostly in search of some answers for myself. Answers that would help me understand my episodes of seeing odd crafts and beings, and my having knowledge of things that your average person had no clue about. That's why this searching was so essential, I just had to find out what was going on with me and my so called "connections" to these odd occurrences.

I began on my quest of answers quite innocently one day while walking through my neighborhood mall when I was 16. I had never gone into a bookstore before really, I figured I had enough to read at school so why torture myself any further in my free time. But as so many others have claimed before, I had a mind-opening experience when I came across the book cover of Whitley Strieber's *Communion*. The book was sitting in the display window in this bookstore and I didn't even know what it was about. I just knew that I would have to come back with some money on my next trip to the mall, to buy it.

I honestly cannot say that the drawing on this book cover of a Gray alien being with large, almond-shaped eyes, looked familiar to me at all. But after finally reading the book about Strieber's life of terrorizing alien encounters, I had a sort of awakening. I got drawn into the notion that I needed to continue to seek out more information on this UFO and alien topic. I somehow knew that I was about to get on the right path to finding out who I really was and why strangeness seemed to follow me.

This path led me to expand on my hunger for more knowledge where I felt the need to read even more books. I began to watch any and all television specials and eventually I even joined groups that all dealt with the subject of UFO's. It was during this time of seeking that I began to realize more and more, that I was a willing part of something bigger than I could ever have imagined.

This investigative stage of seeking out information was nothing compared to what presented to me personally, aside from outside sources. In recent years, doors began flying open left and right to an unending amount of knowledge that I cannot and do not want to close. It is all too much a part of who I am, and my meaning for being. Much of this accessible knowledge came to me by way of teachings, in what I tend to call "night school."

Night school is a place that some alien contactees are taken to in order to exchange knowledge or really, be reminded about how to do some things with different types of beings. This is generally experienced during the night, where the person either leaves physically or spiritually from their beds. I remember teachings being done in settings directly on UFO craft, and various other environments. Whatever place was suitable for a teaching, you would experience just what was needed whether it was in a park or underwater somewhere.

I can even recall being taken to a different kind of night school, a more spiritual place where there were ancient Roman-like buildings all around. But the buildings were made of a sparkling white crystal with a hue of light blue that had small, white lights in it. There were always many figures walking around too, that had long white robes on. One time I was being led by one of the robed figures who took me in front of a crystal scroll on a pedestal, which had names inscribed on it.

I asked if my name was on the scroll and the figure replied, "No. Not yet. But soon it will be."

I was then led inside one of the buildings and sat down on a single long stretch of carved-like bleacher seating formed in a half-circle around, in a single large room. I knew there were others in the room but I could not see them, I was too focused on what was being said by the instructor in the front of this room.

I don't recall exactly what the instructor looked like and I am never quite sure of what is taught in these sessions either. After I return it's like I have all the answers to everything in the universe, only to have someone come along and wipe the chalkboard clean in my mind. That can be very frustrating at times, but I also know that I have those teachings in me somewhere to access when needed.

For me personally, when I go to night school it's not something that I am taken to kicking and screaming either, as so many describe being a part of their abduction experiences with aliens. This is not an abductee story that I am relaying. I go along because I am a part of these places I travel to. I have never felt that I was a victim of any sort, even when I could not recollect what would happen to me in my contacts. In being aware of this, I just knew there was something more to my experiences than most others that I had heard or read of. But to say I knew all along to what extent I was involved, would be far from the truth.

Now I know what some might think when they hear this kind of talk of eagerly going along with some non-human beings like it comes so naturally and without fear. Most think of it as some kind of weird spiritual hub-bub of some wacky folks on drugs or something. If those that think that way have been keeping up on the related stories of alien contact, this idea of "volunteering" and being willing participants of contact, would be old news.

Many people who have had experiences with alien beings are now suddenly realizing that they volunteered to be a part of whatever it is they are experiencing. Some people are coming to these conclusions by way of hypnosis or simply just by a strong sense of *knowing*. I for one can relate to that strong sense, because that is what really helped me to realize my involvement with non-human beings.

Deep inside I knew I had a direct link somehow, it was almost as if I was born with this natural instinct to search for a missing segment in my life. I can remember even as a 5 year child, that I felt I needed to take the time to search some things out about myself, that I was in someways different from most. But I somehow had it instilled in my mind that I had to be careful on my searching so I wouldn't draw too much attention to myself. That I had to be aware and alert so I wouldn't be caught somehow.

Now as a child I didn't know that what I was being aware for was government and alien connected, but now as an adult I know just what it was that I was taking heed of. I was constantly being given scenarios, whether it was in dreams or brief moments of day dreaming, on what to do if I ever did get caught.

"Caught in doing what though?" I'd often throw that question around to myself.

But in actuality I knew exactly what it was on the inside, but couldn't put it all into words. I also knew that I had to keep my suspicions to myself that I was somehow different. But being a child I would often slip up and reveal my differences at times by asking things like, "Why do we have to put one foot in front of the other? This takes forever, it's much faster to fly!" and "Where does fat go when you lose it?"

As you can see from my inquires, I had a slightly different perspective of reality than most kids, and I knew it. But what can you do about it? I know my mom got creative in answering those kinds of questions though by saying things like, "Fat floats in the air and lands on children that ask odd questions." Needless to say, I lived in terror of fat nailing me at any given moment.

But back to my point, when a person has a self-realization that they are in touch with *something else*, you'd think a whole lot of things could be made available to that person then, right? Well any logical thinking person might see it that way anyhow. Now then, when after years you finally are able to fit the pieces and relate that "something else" with a name like "aliens," then you really have something to work with!

Just think of it, "You know that you have a direct connection with aliens." Now then try saying that over and over, that kind of revelation can really shine a light on every dark corner in your mind.

Okay, so now you know the whole scoop about *who* you are and *why* you are, right? You would probably feel like you are about to explode with this information, you surely don't want to just keep it to yourself.

But just how do you show others what you have realized, experienced and what you mean? It's nearly impossible to go and relate something like that to a regular person that is all into the "here and now" and what their hair looks like in the morning.

When I was fully awakened to my involvement with all of this other-worldly stuff, it was no small matter. At the exact moment it happened too, I wasn't even trying to consciously gain the information either. But it was nothing I wanted to be quiet about, yet I knew that it was something most could not grasp, making it nearly impossible to freely speak on it:

It was sometime in May of 1997, I was sitting on my deep-purple futon talking to my roommate and friend I'll just call, Amanda. We were in fact discussing a paranormal experience we had both just had when I decided to get up to go make a visit to the bathroom. I casually stood up and took a couple of steps forward, when my eyes suddenly were flooded with this powerful vision.

I quickly found myself gazing on a scene in space, and there I was! I saw myself as a ball of white light leaving a huge beautiful light, that I somehow knew to be called "The Source." I knew that I was leaving this light so that I may come here to be born to literally complete a mission, of all things! I also had the strong intention in mind that I would come back to The Source to report in, so to speak, on how it all went. The vision left me as quickly as it had come, but I was still left with this knowledge of **knowing** it was real.

I can't really say it was a vision though because to me it really was a time of reflection, a memory even. It was a memory so strong, I was totally overwhelmed with emotions and began to tear a bit. I think that shocked me the most because I am not an emotional person at all, my tears usually only come forward when I see great acts of kindness, oddly enough. The pain that others inflict are not as moving as love to me, I suppose that's why it effects me more in that manner than cruelty does.

Upon seeing this wondrous sight, I slowly began to back up to sit down on my futon and I just kept repeating sluggishly over and over, "Whoa, whoa, whoa!"

Amanda didn't know what to think, she just kept asking me, "What's wrong, what's going on?!"

Then I started to repeat, "How could I have forgotten?!"

I practically felt ashamed of my lack of remembrance. In seeing this vision of this place, it was like equivalent to forgetting my first name or something! I can't forget my first name, so how could I forget about this place then?! To me it was just totally absurd to forget something so essential about myself and here I forgot truly *who* I was and am!

I went on to describe to Amanda how I remembered everything in my coming here to be on Earth. I told her, "It was as if my memory was sitting just out in front of my forehead," and I positioned my hand out in front of my head. "And "they" let me have it only for a minute just to remind me of who I was and that I was on the right path."

I went on to tell her that I saw what many call the Library of Knowledge or Akashic Records just above this swirling mass of beautiful light that was called The Source. The Source is what I would compare to the likes of God, the beginning of beginnings, a mass consortium of many spirits to equal one.

Me along with trillions of souls in it flowed clockwise, in the same direction as you could see the light spinning. Ideas, thoughts, and decisions flowed through the light like a gentle wave of water and all of the souls gave their input into it as it passed by. The thought passed through about a mission that needed to be done and for one reason or another, I quickly volunteered. As soon as I did I shot out of there so fast and direct, in a blink of an eye. Then I immediately felt overcome by a terrible and overwhelming feeling of anxiety from the detachment from this rich love soup of light and wanted to return instantly back to The Source.

But I knew that was not possible and I knew where I was headed. I was to go off to be trained for this mission I'd volunteered for, and this training would take place in various locations that I have described as night school and other lifetimes. But before even being human and going in the nights with other beings, I was trained and lived with many different kinds of beings. I was even incarnated on one planet that was going through the same events Earth is now, so that I may have the background to understand what I am up against here.

Back in my instance of recalling where I came from, I also remembered that right there above and to the left of The Source (if you are looking at it from here), is the Library of Knowledge. I really don't have a name for it, all I know is that this is where all the records are kept of anything and everything there ever was or is. How I knew all about what I had just seen, baffled me to the extreme. It was just like remembering my old stomping grounds or backyard. I just knew what everything was and the purpose of everything, and it came so naturally.

So there I was, sitting there in awe and trying to explain to Amanda the magnitude of what just happened to me. I had never quite experienced such a thing like that before, and I felt sort of dumbfounded because I felt no explanation I could give was efficient enough. I had just seen **God** for crying out loud, that sort of thing is just a little difficult to reenact!

"How could I really show her what I just saw, aside from just words?" I thought to myself.

So I figured, "I'm somewhat of an artist, I'll draw it for her."

I sat down and got my colored pencils out and did the best rendition I could do in a very brief amount of time. But of course, I still couldn't do it justice. It's a good thing Amanda had her fair share of seeing things not of this realm too, so she had no problem in believing me from the start.

But when it came time for me to try and explain this grand ordeal to some other friends, I had no words for them. I knew they wouldn't get it, so I just kept it inside my other network of close friends who were experiencers of the odd sort also. But it really saddened me to know that regular everyday people just sometimes cannot open up to the possibilities of other things.

How did we as children explain to our parents that you didn't break the vase that you heard crash to the floor in another room when no one else was in the house but you? I know when that happened to me, I couldn't convince them. But I knew the truth, still in all of my pleading it fell on deaf ears and I still had to pay for that vase.

There is nothing I can do to prove anything to anyone, I just hope that my truths are taken into some consideration and maybe you will see them as some kind of hint of truth also. If my pleads do not reach you in reading this book, it is not something that I will be at a loss for. I won't have to pay for the vase this time, thank goodness.

I am hoping that no one will have to pay for not knowing the true reality of our universe and this is the challenge I have decided to take on and I do so with pride and caution. I want to make sure that I explain myself and intentions clearly so as not to be misleading nor confusing.

Often you may see that I take a humorous stand point in relating some concepts. But I do not do this to make light of the topics at all, it's just that some of the things I have to lay out are truly heavy and it helps to lighten the load if we can all just laugh a bit. So bear this all in mind as I attempt to reveal and relate the complicated stories that have been told to me by some alien friends that I like to consider as family.

2

AMANDA: *A NEW CONTACT BEGINS*

I'm sure that one of the first things people would think of if they had a connection to aliens is the technology that could be made available to them, and some people are being given that. Others might think of the endless traveling they could enjoy aboard a space craft, and that tends to happen too. Then there's the other possibility that maybe you can really learn what aliens and their agenda on Earth is all about, and obviously that's the one thing that I have been chosen to do. But I am not alone on this journey.

My friend that I mentioned earlier, Amanda, is very much a part of my understandings of alien beings. Amanda, also happens to be an artist too, but about 100 times better than I am. She and I got along great as roommates since she also happened to specialize in drawing cartoons, which is what I do too. So needless to say our place was a bit colorful with cartoony and artsy themes all about.

In someways I think artists are more sensitive to paranormal things. We seem to pay closer attention to details and things that are generally overlooked by others. We always seem to seek out beauty in every crevasse, and while in our searching we often stumble across other things. Well I can say with certainty that Amanda is one that stumbles, and profusely at that.

By now most people have heard that when people are in the presence of alien beings, they communicate telepathically. Meaning, they speak to your mind directly without verbal communication, and some people speak back to them in the same manner. If you can conceive of this being possible, then what other way might you imagine they would be able to communicate?

Well channeling, believe it or not, and that happens to be another source for this book. That word alone conjures up ideas of sorcery, witchcraft or whatever dark and mystical practices there are. But this is not that sort of dealing, there are some elements to it that are way different when it concerns the beings communicating in this fashion.

When in the presence of different alien beings, whether on a ship or wherever, they think a thought and poof it's in your head. With this channeling form I'm speaking of it's very similar, they think the thought and it can just pop into your head. But your own mouth can also be used to relay the message to others they may want to hear the message too. The person channeling doesn't have to open their mouth to get what's being said to them, they can keep it to themselves. Sometimes the beings can be present too, or not, to get this across. So to think that telepathic communication is far-out, channeling is no more weirder, even practically the same.

Channeling is the gift that Amanda was surprised to find that she possessed, but she likes to consider it meditation or prayer since that was where she found alien beings waiting to communicate with her. Why these two words work the same for her is because she has always prayed in a meditative state. In all honesty prayer is a form of mediation. But when Amanda has taken this approach prior to the incident I am about to detail, she did not go into prayer for any other reasons than any of us do, to speak to God.

As she and I ventured on with this talent of hers, we also learned that this channeling gift was not totally Amanda's either. You could say she kind of meets "them" half-way and they use a form of technology to complete the connection.

She feels better knowing this because she says she does not feel so odd to say that it is just all her doing this weird channeling thing. For some reason she thinks since it is partially technology, that she will not lose herself and identity in talking with different beings too much. She and I have both heard of channelers that do not use their gift of channeling anymore just because they felt they were becoming too blended with the entities they spoke with.

Amanda's case of speaking with non-human beings is a very unique one in that she came across her first entity quite by accident, and you would think would have caused an accident too. I can't help but to go into this story a bit, because it really shows how seemingly everyday people are totally drawn into this sort of thing whether they liked the topic or not. Amanda was one who totally did not care for the topic of UFO's or aliens and pretty much had to get shaken up a bit before she acknowledged what was going on around her.

From the time when Amanda first moved in with me she lived with me for about 1 1/2 years before she finally came to grips with her alien connection. Before she moved in, I told her that I often had strange phenomena going on in the house. I wanted to make sure she knew fully what she was moving into and would not be startled too badly when odd things would happen or appear. I told her about the odd electrical happenings, things moving on their own and your occasional walk through of some see-through visitors and so on, just your typical contactee home.

Well she confided in me that she would have no problem with that because she had God on her side, so therefore my demons would not be able to touch her.

"Demons?" I said.

"Well then if you see my little *demons* running around then, you just ignore them ok?" I told her. She agreed and moved on in anyway.

Well, it took only a few weeks for her to see that my demons were not demons at all when she witnessed three of them hanging around one day. In fact she could see them more clearly than I could! To me I could just see outlines and shapes, but she could see the eyes and details of all of them very well.

Doing what artists do, she then proceeded to draw me what she was seeing so we could compare drawings, since I was doing the same. Of course our drawings coincided. But another interesting thing occurred too where she could also sense that they had no evil intentions. But for one reason or another, she still felt more comfortable in calling them demons instead of aliens, go figure.

Since that time Amanda bore witness to many other phenomena, but she still had a hard time accepting the fact of what she was experiencing.

"I want to see a UFO," she would contend over and over, "and then I'd know for sure what they are."

She wouldn't get that wish of her's for sometime either, and I suppose it took too long because she started to denounce everything she ever saw in relation to the topic. In fact, aliens and UFO's was a topic that became banned from all conversation with her unless she was making fun of it. She then began to blend with the rest of my friends, since poking fun of the topic was typical of them. So once again I had only my friends involved in the UFO groups to turn to when I'd have an astonishing encounter or experience. It was a shame that I had to go so far to speak to someone instead of being able to look over my shoulder to share it with those that were closest to me.

But then in April of 1997, Amanda was paid a special visit while driving to college one day, and the time must have been right:

The phone rang and I went to answer it, "Heidi, oh my God!" I recognized it as being Amanda and she was crying hysterically. "Heidi, I don't know, something flew in my windshield and started talking to me and now it's in my class! I can't stop shaking, it's like shocking me or something…oh my God it's here again!" She then continued to cry.

I completely had no clue what she was talking about. She sounded like she was having a breakdown or something, not that she had ever before. But I offered to pick her up and drive her home so she could settle down.

In the midst of all her sobbing and tears she surprised me when she said, "No, no I'm ok! It-it, feels good!"

She described that there was a being she was seeing and it was shocking her full of what felt to her as strong, positive energy. She said she just wished that her hands would stop shaking so she could continue to draw in her art class. She was a bit self-conscious that the others in her class would think she was having a seizure or something! So to avoid any strange stares, she decided to leave class early that day.

Later that evening when she got back from school, we went out driving around by Milwaukee's eastside by Lake Michigan. She then began to tell me in more detail what had happened to her earlier that day. She described to me how this clear, see-through being full of sparkles peered through her windshield while she was driving to school, thus my reason for concern for her in having an accident. She said she just automatically started relating to this being and talking to it.

I asked her if she got scared or freaked out, since she would often scream out when she would have night visits by different beings. Aliens can be so abrupt in visiting people. I don't think some of them understand that they have the element of surprise on their side that causes our hearts to do back-flips even though some may mean no harm.

Amanda went on to tell me, "No. It was weird, it had a real calming effect to it. What really surprised me was when it answered me back, it would use my mouth!"

She said it felt like when she would have her mouth numbed at the dentist. But then she felt her mouth moving really stiff-like, just snapping up and down like a puppet!

She recalled asking the being, "Who are you and what is your purpose here?"

The being responded, "What humans call an alien. Each of us has a specific part to do in this mission and we will often change off to serve our individual purposes."

Amanda then had the idea pass through her mind that he was like the initiator of contact, a sort of ambassador to start relations.

Amanda then began to rattle off questions at the being as if she had rehearsed them or something. When I think about it, she really did have a lot of time to accumulate questions since she had been experiencing many things right along with me for some time. But unlike myself, she would never let herself vent her concerns. So I suppose when this being made itself available she just let it flow.

Amanda continued on to ask, "Some people think you guys are here to either destroy the planet or help it out. So then what are you doing here anyways?"

"We will not be the ones to destroy the Earth. The humans will, and when they have done so we will be here to help those that survive," the being responded.

"You mean just like my dream? That's what it's going to be like when all this ends?"

Amanda had a dream three days earlier that she was trying to relate to, and I will go into more detail about that in chapter #4. But in brief, Amanda's dream showed her our planet in destruction.

"Humans only live by emotions. They only respond to something they are experiencing at the moment, they do not see the direct damage they are causing. It will be too late by the time they realize their fate." The being explained.

Then the being went on about more personal matters, "It is not a coincidence you met Heidi and are now studying about the Indians. Nothing is ever a coincidence."

Amanda was taking a class at the time, that spoke about the beliefs the Native Americans had. In reading over some of the text books, she and I both discovered that the Native Americans had a lot of what sounded to us like alien encounters. So much in fact, that Amanda focused on that concept for her final project and presentation.

Amanda presented to her class how they may have indeed had contact and that their beliefs surrounded around other-worldly visitations. Some of the Native American's lore directly stated that they were given their instructions by the gods of the sky. These instructions included how to respect the environment, all the way to how they performed rituals to dance until exhaustion so their bodies became weak and easier to leave so they could have experiences and/or visions of the beings and spirits. By this sparkling-being mentioning the "Indians," I guess we were right to think what we did about the Native American's beliefs.

While Amanda was speaking of what she experienced earlier that day, I continued to listen in amazement to her account. We soon had stopped driving and had parked near the lake to continue to chat. Then suddenly Amanda reveals something that I would have never expected, she told me she felt the urge to meditate right then and there. I had never witnessed her meditate or pray before. In fact she had never done this in front of anyone aside from guided relaxation, so it was pretty odd for her to volunteer this outright. But who was I to say no, finally my best friend was getting hip to this UFO stuff so I let her lead the way.

When Amanda began to meditate, I had no idea that a whole new world would open up to us. There was someone waiting for us on the other side of her mind's eye. Something warm, friendly and inviting. Just patiently waiting for us to tap in, so that we may open our eyes and the quite possibly, the world's.

3

CAFTH SPEAKS: *THE INTRODUCTION*

When Amanda answered her urge to meditate right then at the lake front, she had no choice from then on but to acknowledge her connection with aliens. The funny part is, after all the scrutiny and ridicule I took from her and now suddenly she was in tune with this supposed "strange stuff."

That first night when Amanda and I were sitting in the car along Lake Michigan, she in trance, and I an eager onlooker, my ears were flooded with info about our place within the universe.

I was about to get my first direct lesson from a source I could not see that claimed to have the answers that we were looking for concerning all of our strange happenings. Ends that we thought could never be tied, and here, suddenly they were about to.

There was a feeling of openness and oneness that came over me that night at Lake Michigan. If I didn't know any better I would think I was sitting in a souped-up convertible with the top down so that I was able to gaze up to the stars. But I wasn't. We were sitting in my raggedy-bucket of a car with rust spots creeping up the doors ever so slightly. No there was nothing magical about where I was, it was all about who was there.

I had in the back of mind, what Amanda had explained about the being that visited her earlier that day. How I wished I had been there to see this being and the look on her face when it made it's entrance into her car. But I would soon get to meet whom it was that being was making way for, everything always happens in due time.

An alien being came through Amanda and greeted us, called us by name and then referred to us as part of his family. Family of all things, no wonder I felt such a comfortable sense of awe about me in that tight little space.

Amanda's posture had changed and her usual Spanish accent reduced. The being then began moving Amanda's lips by saying first, "I have been waiting to speak to you for a very long time."

I was a bit stunned, but not too much to where my thoughts were in a bind, so I let my mind and questions surge forward. I was curious as to who was talking and so I asked the being what it's name was, then Amanda herself came through and explained that she was seeing a triangle with a line through it. I asked her what that meant to her, then the being came back and spelled slowly, C-A-F-T-H.

I then pronounced this name out loud and it said, "Ugh, I hate the way your human mouths form my name!"

I wanted to say, "Well excuse me!" But I found it pretty funny and laughed at this Cafth character.

But, I of course did not take what was happening lightly. I mean here is my best friend in trance, appearing to have an impressive being speaking through her. Sure, it ran through my head that maybe she was pulling the biggest prank of her life off at my expense. But then I recalled the phone call and the sincerity of her tears pouring out over the phone. Then here we sat talking in-depth when she urgently feels the need to drop into meditation which was something she had never offered to do in front of anybody before.

"Bonnie did this sort of thing in front of me and several others before. This is really happening Heidi, just let it!" I thought emphatically to myself.

I had witnessed something like this before, where an alien being spoke up through another friend of mine, who I'll just call Bonnie. But that time it did not happen while sitting alone with just that person in trance, in a small space. I admit, I was a bit spooked out by it in spurts. But then I thought of my friend who was also alone in this too. I had to find a way to drag up the courage to explore this thing with her further. Besides that,

about to have a Q & A session with these ever evasive
g .... so drawn to learn about for so long.

I took a deep breath and pushed on to ask Cafth my first of many questions by asking where he was.

He responded, "In a ship very high up."

I asked if he could show us his ship now and he said, "We can no longer come in very close as often as we could before, because now your government's have our technology to track us."

I asked him how did they get their technology and he continued, "Many of our ships have crashed, so they now know how to penetrate our ships to shoot us down, so we don't come down as much now."

I have heard countless stories of people seeing UFO craft being chased by military planes as if they were trying to lock onto them to shoot them down. But what was the purpose of all this? Were the UFO occupants being threatening or were they just simply a threat because they were in our air space? I could never quite figure out why the governments on this planet considered these other-worldly beings to be such a threat. Those answers would be given to me later, but the reasons were nothing I would have ever expected.

Cafth continued on to tell me that he could, however, project himself down to the surface at times when he was close enough.

I asked him, "Well then, can you show yourself now?"

"Can't you see me now?" Cafth came back.

The car then seemed to fill with a warm hum and I turned closer towards Amanda at this point and asked, "Where?"

Then I pulled myself back a little from the drivers seat where Amanda was sitting. Then just ever so faintly, I could make out a brownish-fleshy colored, smokey figure right next to her between the two of us. I was a bit taken by seeing it, but it was hard to make out and I told him so. But he said it could not be helped because for one, he was too high up and two, I had weak human eyes! I suppose being human makes our eyes limited to their wavelength, who knows.

Once when my friend Bob was being regressed, he had a hard time describing anything he was seeing too, the beings, his surroundings, nothing.

Then he suddenly realized, "I know why I can't recognize anything. We've been taken out of our time. They can do that!"

Now I could understand better what he meant and see why I could not see Cafth clearly, nor some other entities I have encountered at times. They just exist in another time and it is hard to translate that time into our own. We just don't know what we are seeing, nor how to relate it to something because we have not experienced these things before, or so we think.

After the initial shock of seeing Cafth and then fading away, he continued to reveal more and referred to me as family. He said, "Your mother was not your mother, we needed her DNA to sustain you. When she felt she had achieved her goals she asked to be taken, so we came and got her."

Let me tell you, after a statement like that, there were a million and one things running through my head! My mom had died due to head injuries in a car accident in 1978, she lost control of her car when she suffered a heart attack. I had always wondered about the coincidences of her passing. Two weeks or so before she died, it was as if she knew her fate and had prepared me and my younger sister. She spoke to us in detail on what to do and what not to do in the event of her death. She had no pre-existing health factors at the age of 47 to make her state what she did, but there was no mistaking her timing.

Amanda knows how tragic that loss was to me and she personally would never bring up the subject, nor suggest anything close to what this Cafth being was saying. So I figured it must be really important that this was ever brought up, so I continued to pursue the topic.

I asked, "So you mean to tell me that my mom is up there riding around in a UFO with you and other aliens or something?"

"Yes she is, in her human spirit form."

"So what does that make me?!"

"Alien. But human for now. Your mother's human DNA made your body for your essence to be held in."

He further explained that those people that don't have fully human souls, need to have bodies that can handle their presence. It's not a breeding program as many know of the Gray beings getting involved with creating half-human and half-alien hybrid children. It's essentially timing, with slight modifications, to ensure the body can hold-up and contain a non-human essence. I was baby number eight my mom had, so it seems it took some time to get the right balance of what was needed.

Honestly though, I was not totally blown away by what he said. My inner voice had already told me who I was a long time ago as a child. But at this time, it would still be a month before I would have my vision of The Source and Library of Knowledge I've mentioned. To have private thoughts of who I was, was one thing, but to hear the finer details of my whole make-up come from an outer source was still a shocker. I had not ever revealed my true suspicions of having other origins to anyone before him saying this. In my book thus far, Cafth was no joke.

At this point, things started to get a bit more involved and odd sounding. It would be wise to hold tight and try to follow along closely with what will be explained next. To many, a great portion of this next material might not make immediate sense. But I'm hoping to some extent, some of it will stick to mind.

It can be very difficult to relate and balance the information there is to know and learn in two different realms of reality. It is also very hard to transfer the knowledge to spell it out to someone in one dimension over another too. I wish I were able to just come and hand someone a solid object that can do weird feats to prove to them that the other reality exists. But doing that would create almost like followers, and anyone who would want that I'd suggest to be leery of.

We all trust the scientists when they say there are radio waves in the air even though we can't see them, but we do see the end result so they must be there. Well trust in this in what I am saying, that there are other things out there that our scientists are just as able to measure (but deny) that exist too, and the results are everywhere and not as elusive as many may think.

But there is no easy, nor simple way to put this all down, so I am just going to tell it as it is:

I am, what I have been told on several occasions by strangers and friends, as being a form of a "light being." This is the form that I saw myself in when I had the vision of arriving here to complete a mission of some kind. But I did learn that a better name to describe me was as an "energy being," that of which I lack while in this form. No energy, that is. I cannot recall ever really having a hyper day in my life. I have since learned that I lack in energy because I no longer have access to the light energy that I fed off from at one time from The Source and other things. Probably much like how we as humans take in certain vitamins from the sun here.

So in-turn and quite frequently in fact, I blow out things like street lights, computers and other gizmos when I am in their vicinity. You could say that these things turn off the way they do because I use them as a nutritional supplement instead of the light I used to have access to, if I'm understanding correctly. But I also notice these things happen when I'm running high on emotions like being overly happy or a bit down. But doing things like that are also a characteristic of others that are in contact with non-human beings too. So it's good to know that I am not the only one, and that it applies to others with various kinds of ties.

As strange as this may all sound, it even goes deeper. At a later date Cafth told me how he and some others had rescued me and seven others from my place of origin, a planet, before something happened to it. They would not tell me exactly what happened, because they did not want me to dwell on that now. But as I mentioned before, I knew that this first planet was a place for me to learn from. Cafth said when I was brought to him I was nothing but a small spark of light, and I was pretty much raised and trained by Cafth and the others on the ship. I became a part of their family, and they taught me all I would need to know for my mission and important cause here on Earth. Now, much of this I do recall, or have a deep knowing to be true.

been said. It's strange to read on paper, but not so strange in my memories. I'm also not so odd and rare either, because there are plenty of others here already that are not completely of this Earth. Many are sharing what they recall even, but others just don't know how to explain what they truly know about themselves.

Take Amanda's story for instance, she was shown how she was brought to Cafth by a more spiritual being by the name of Soforus. Amanda was really shocked to find that these two beings knew each other at all, she had known of Soforus sometime before hand.

It was sometime in 1996, Amanda had tried to be hypnotically regressed to remember a time when she first saw aliens in her bedroom as a child (she admitted at a later date to seeing aliens before but still related them as demons). Instead of retrieving a memory, she found herself being taken through various blue tunnels by this being, Soforus.

Blue tunnels that I, in my attempt to be regressed one time, saw also. But I was blocked at the entrance by a dark shadowy figure that grew into many, so I did not get to enter the tunnels. Amanda had not known about my experience either before she went on speaking about the many different places these blue tunnels led her to. She was pleased to hear about my sighting of the tunnels after her experience in them though. It's always a good feeling to know that you are not alone in any of these kinds of experiences.

In both experiences for Amanda in 1996 and 1997, first Soforus, then Cafth showed Amanda her true form as being a brightly lit ball of light, one that changed colors and grew in size as it matured. Her kind of beings lived somewhere near Soforus and his blue tunnels, that he said he was the keeper of. Soforus had brought her to Cafth when she was underdeveloped so she could be taught as I was, but at different levels. So together we were both taught various things to help on this dire mission we are now supposed to be in the middle of.

So here we are.

"What's next?" I'd often wonder. So now thanks to Cafth and Soforus and our memories, we both knew who we were and that we were on a mission. But a mission of what in mind?! I had to learn to be patient, because all in due time our answers would surface. But for now, now it was time to contemplate our first contact and conversation with Cafth.

After her first true line of communication was opened that night with Cafth, Amanda just couldn't move her mouth fast enough to ask me all she could think of on the topic of aliens. She was on such a roll, she almost got me to the point of laughing hysterically. She had wasted so much time poking fun at the topic, that she lacked how to go about understanding exactly what was going on.

Upon getting home from the lake front that evening, she picked up and started reading about five of my books on the subject of aliens, all at once! For her, this reading frenzy was a feat in itself since she's Puerto Rican and does not like to read English writing very much. I of course, had to have a little fun with it all since she had limited me so much in our conversations in the past. So in the beginning of this contact time with Cafth, I would question her if she was sure she was sane. I'd let her know I had never had anything quite like that happen to me, so I didn't know about all this being normal behavior or not.

I'm bad.

Actually though, as I had mentioned in brief before, we both had a mutual friend named Bonnie that had similar experiences. Amanda and I had in fact witnessed this kind of channeling contact on several occasions with her. Bonnie was someone I had confided in while pursuing my interests in the UFO topic, who then later found her talents in channeling quite by accident too.

In the past, Amanda had her suspicions about Bonnie and her whole channeling bit. Amanda just could not understand how it was possible for an alien to even exist, let alone speak through someone. But now suddenly, this had all subsided once Cafth came along and she had a lot of questions for Bonnie too.

To explain a little more on Bonnie, I don't know what the odds are of this, but she so happened to come across her talents when I was present also. She was attempting to be regressed to remember some instances of missing time in her life, and myself and several others were present at Bonnie's home while she was having this done. It was then when a being by the name of Kolis suddenly came through and spoke up in a simple tone of voice. We knew something was up with Bonnie when she started giggling and pointing at her body parts and was unable to form words properly.

We especially took a hint when her daughter said something to the effect like, "Uh, that's not my mom ya guys!"

In this first contact session, it took several minutes for the being Kolis to even sound out a simple word, and this went on for hours! I have now heard of several instances where a contactee has tried to be regressed by hypnosis and out comes an alien entity speaking for them instead. Amanda came by it in a different form, but I think it was easier for her to go about this sort of thing through meditation. I say this because for as long as she can recall, she had always done prayer in the form of meditation in this manner her entire life.

It seems that any form of meditation is the key here to help open up ourselves to the bigger picture and truth of things, but this is not an easy feat for everyone. Personally I have found it difficult to maintain myself in meditation for long periods of time. But it's important to note, that I have still been able to see things for what they are for myself with my eyes open.

It seems that I have always had some sort of a block that has limited me from having a full meditational connection for some reason. I also have not been fully successful to go *down* with hypnosis to retrieve any memories either, but I still do receive information by a different means. When Amanda meditates or channels, at times I can also see who it is she is speaking to and the setting they are in. I suppose that is a form of channeling, but it is a gift I have always possessed but never tested before until Amanda began her channeling bit.

For me, this gift kind of worked out on its own without my full knowledge of being there. Ever listen to someone talking to you about something or some place they have been and you picture it all in your head happening as they say it? Well I did that too, but at times I would step in and mention something the person forgot to describe. Every once and awhile I did this sort of thing, purely by accident, until I thought there might be something to this. Especially when the other person would exclaim there was no way I could know what it was they experienced or saw.

So when Amanda started doing her channeling, my pictures would also come through pretty strong, and keep in mind that these images come through while my eyes are wide open and talking. I was lucky to have this extra insight on my side, so that way I could truly see what it was Amanda was getting at when she was trying to describe what she was witnessing sometimes.

Then there are the episodes where I would get a tingling sensation throughout my body and hear like the electricity in the air change frequency or something, then messages or ideas would just drop in my head. Some of these messages were so foreign that I knew they could not have come from anywhere but outside of myself. Plus, some of the night school lessons that are on the outskirts of my mind are often brought forward by revelations brought up by Cafth too.

There's just so many alternatives and differences in how any one person is able to gain access to some form of spiritual insight. I really don't think there is any one best way for anybody to tap into the *something else*. Whatever works for an individual, and it feels right, I say trust it and go with it. If you are suspicious that whatever you are getting in your psyche is somehow coming from outside yourself, well then that feeling's there for a reason, we all can't be crazy.

So with all this in mind, one should be able to tell that the contents of this book are not just taken from Amanda's lips as living scripture, that would sound too cult-like. No, a lot of the information being discussed, has also been experienced or witnessed by myself and some of our friends. These are the same friends that have witnessed the presences that come along with and coincide with Amanda's channelings and other related experiences that have helped shed some light along the way. Experiences that have at times been very difficult to decipher, that is, until the time was right for us to solve or figure it out. There were so many riddles that needed to be solved, and in being faced with the opportunity before me with Amanda's new gift, I would be foolish to not make use of what was being presented.

I began to explore some subjects with Cafth to get a feel for what information and answers I could actually get from this contact. One topic I especially wanted to touch on was about some odd experiences that began to expand upon itself in my home on an almost daily basis for the past three or more years. Previously, I would often have things like lights in various shapes and colors, smokey apparitions, and sometimes even outlines of see-through forms drop by the house. These were a more common occurrence, but a newer more peculiar presence began to stop by once too often.

I soon became more aware that these peculiar things were actually a being of some sort. They were generally large and very tall too, but they could range anywhere from a small blob to approximately 10 feet tall. Their whole appearance could only be made out to what looked like a large black shadow with a rounded head directly connected to it's shoulders, without a neck to be seen. These things sometimes put the icing on the cake by glaring at me and making their slanted, or round, red eyes apparent.

It's really something to be met with a huge monstrous black thing only to see eyes develop and peer down at you. There have been times where I truly thought that my legs would fall out from under me while standing face to face with one of these creatures. But I somehow managed to get through, and I mean that literally I have had to go through them to get to an exit that they blocked off!

Whatever they were, they were a nuisance and horrifying to wake up to or bump into while fully conscious. One explicable element to experiencing these beings presence was how I generally got to see them. I mostly recognized them in a room by way of my side or peripheral vision, but not exclusively. For a while I could never understand why it was that I could see these apparitions more clearly in my peripheral vision either. But I later learned that it's easier to see things of this sort from the side because our peripheral vision is more sensitive to differences in lights and dark.

It was almost as if these beings lurked in the dark in hopes they would be overlooked. But I saw them alright, sometimes I am sure of it that they purposely stepped out from the shadows to invoke a respectful fear out of me. Well they had the fear part right, but respect for causing that was a bit off. I began to see those big shadowy things so much that I even picked out a reflective name of their character, the "Shadow People."

I sensed these Shadow People as being very nosey and watchful of what I was doing. They didn't feel as passive as most of the entities I would encounter in my home either. No, these beings were a lot more intrusive.

As I became more and more aware of myself and other-worldly things, the presence of these Shadow People increased as well. I grew a bit concerned about this and began to finally mention the presence of these beings to my friends. All I really mentioned to them was the part about these beings being really nosey and that they had a negative feel to them. I didn't have any answers about this phenomena, but as always, some light would be shed on this mystery in due time.

There came a time when me and six of my friends from the M.A.S.E (Mid-west Abductee Support and Enlightenment) group went to Eureka Springs, Arkansas for their annual UFO conference. On the trip down there in April of 1995, we experienced some odd things that included my friend Jim being severely burned by no normal means. Several batteries in a radio he had on his lap exploded and caused a 1/4 inch deep chemical burn on his leg where a full nickel could fit into it. Yet, he was not aware of the burn until we arrived to our destination a long while later.

So of course this needed further investigation, and we all attempted to be hypnotized. This brings me to my friend Bob again, who went to his therapist's office to be regressed. This particular doctor was someone he had been seeing for some time to try to understand his abduction experiences. He was also accompanied to the office by our mutual friends Bonnie and Jim.

I was not present at the time, because I didn't want to be influenced by his session so that I may attempt to be regressed at a later date myself. But Bob did agree to have his session video taped so I could view it later after my hypnotic attempt. When I did get to view the tape, after I failed at being regressed successfully as always, to my surprise a great deal of what Bob had to say was about me.

He spoke of the Shadow People (calling them by that name) and said how they were trying to get at me to stop me by any means in completing my mission. He said, "Me and Heidi are one of the few travelers left that can accomplish the mission. They're looking for me and they're looking for Heidi!"

He was very upset at this revelation and proceeded to show signs of distress while under hypnosis. He then continued, "They (meaning the beings that had currently taken us) took Heidi to examine her so they could find a way to protect her better."

As I said before, I have always known and felt that I was groomed to be careful and not be caught or stopped in doing what I am here to do. Where this prompting had come from I could not exactly say, but I mostly concentrated on not being found out by some government force not another being though. This all sounds a bit irrate I know, and that is exactly why I never told a soul. I had never liked the idea of trying to bring too much attention to myself, somehow to me that would make me seem as if I was better than others. Then here is this focus of my purpose being so important that there are beings out there to stop me? It was all too very strange.

I'm sure you can imagine, that when I saw the video tape with Bob revealing that there was a threat that I needed to steer clear of, it really caught me off-guard in a way. You know how it is when you have a bad feeling about something like going out with your friends and then you find out later they were in an accident and you could have been seriously hurt?

It's like you got the reinforcement you needed to listen to your inner voice and to continue to listen even closer the next time it's trying to tell you something. That's exactly what Bob's revelation did for me. My gut feelings were trying to say something and they were right.

So there really was something I needed to take heed of and it was something I was doing all along, thank goodness. But this was a being I really didn't know much about consciously, and yet I knew enough to know how to protect myself against these Shadow People to some extent. Whenever there is something that I know that I have no idea how I learned, is when I attribute it to a teaching from night school. Plus I was told that when I needed to know something that I was taught, it would just come to me and that happened all the time.

Well so far I suppose I have been faring pretty well with these Shadow People, my newly founded foe of some sort. As strange as it may seem though, this deal with these Shadow People soon became ordinary and I didn't pay them or the topic much mind for awhile. I did continue to see them though, but I had gotten almost used to their presence and saw no big deal with them anymore. But still the question remained, "What were these Shadow People and why did they want to destroy me?" Of course most everyone sees themselves as being a unique individual, but I didn't feel that impressive to have an enemy from another realm.

Well with Amanda's and my new awakenings, our friends the Shadow People would rear their ugly head around once more. But this time they would come in full force. It seemed the more ahead I got on the subject of aliens, UFO's and my connection with them, the more those things would creep around. I didn't know it then, but soon all my questions would be answered about them and their connection with me and Amanda.

So needless to say, Amanda and I saw some pretty good reasons to continue on our relationship with these newly founded, yet old-friends of ours, Cafth and Soforus. The Shadow People deal was just one small part of what we initially started out to talk to Cafth about, and since Cafth was our main contact we usually directed our questions to him.

There was so much ground to be covered so we tried to get in touch with Cafth whenever we came up with new questions or insights on something. We asked everything from the size of Cafth's ship to why many of them did not wear clothes most of the time. We left no stone unturned, within reason, and with many of our odd questions we found that many of the answers were off limits.

Cafth would often say something like, "It would not benefit you at all to know the answer to that question," or when he felt especially perky he would say something like, "You already know the answer to that." Then his number one all time favorite answer was, "Maybe."

Cafth is quite a character, and he knows it, he seems to get a real kick out of himself sometimes. What gets me is that he accredits me for a lot of his humor. He says that I teach him and other beings all about my favorite human subject, humor, three times a week! I admit, it sounds like something I would do, and it is something I do recall helping to teach at times.

But overall, Cafth proved to me and Amanda that he was more of the "nuts and bolts" contact, he said, "I am here to make sure things are set straight (about the alien presence and purpose on Earth)."

But he is very careful not to push us in one direction over another, he pretty much leaves us hanging to contemplate the topic at hand. I like that too, because then I don't feel as if I am being led around to follow a direct order or something. He said that ultimately we have the choice to listen to what he has to say or not, freewill is always a good thing.

But with our conversations being held more regularly, he has been quite firm on several occasions to state that we were moving too slowly and that our mission was way too important to stall on. I became comfortable enough once to express to him, how I wished myself and Amanda could be blinded to all this stuff so we could just blend in and enjoy whatever life had to offer like everyone else does. It really could become overwhelming to be told some of the things that he was relaying to us about so many issues at times.

In response, Cafth said in an almost sorrowful tone, "Do you know how often we are told that by others? Not everyone takes to our instructions, they forget who they are and what they have come for. We only hope that they will do the right thing and not be caught up in the moment of things."

Cafth really knew how to set us right, even if he didn't mean to directly, and I think me and Amanda have come a long way because of his gentle guidance.

Soforus, on the other hand, dealt with more issues of the spiritual world. Sometimes when Cafth would get a question from us along those lines he would call on Soforus. Then he would just pop in, literally right through the wall of Cafth's ship!

Soforus has been very helpful in answering many questions to help us grasp a lot of spiritual concepts. He himself is also a more spiritual type being too, which may help his understandings more. He does not need a ship to get around in as Cafth does. Cafth looks somewhat similar to the Grays, but has more rounded features such as his eyes and chin. His body is also more defined with some apparent muscular tone and has a flesh-toned color, with a hint of pink. The only striking similarity of the Grays and Cafth, are the large black eyes, but he's quick to say that he is not directly related to the abducting Gray beings who are rather rigid in their appearance with no soft features to speak of.

Soforus on the other hand kind of reminds me of the popular ghost-cartoon character named Casper. He's got a similar body shape as him, but he is a wonderful bright green with deep purple eyes. But I have to point out that he is not at all similar to Cafth when it comes down to having a sense of humor. No sir, Soforus is straight and narrow, yet both he and Cafth share the lack of not understanding human emotions fully.

I know it sounds profound to first hear and learn of aliens existing, then to hear of ones that have personalities on top of it. It has even been hard for me and Amanda to let it sink in that what was happening, was part of our reality now. We had to find a balance where we could breathe and organize in our minds where we stood in our presented existence. It was always a struggle, and it continues to this day at a certain level.

But whenever we seemed to be slacking off on doing things that were in need of getting done regarding our goals here, we would get this extremely strong *urging* feeling to keep us on the right path. For me it g that came externally either, it was more like my soul cry-ing out to me, right in the middle of my chest. I have also spoken to several others who have claimed to get similar feelings of having to do something urgently but they were at a loss of words as to what the project was exactly. It also seemed that whenever I began to feel alone amongst the 6 billion people who reside on this planet and have no clue about any of this, that urging feeling really put me at ease at the same time.

Cafth and Soforus were really an experience to get to know, but little did we know they were warming us up for something. They were trying to prepare us for the truth of the situation all of us are in on this planet, and how they were trying to help out. After Soforus and Cafth began to drop this bomb on me and Amanda slowly and gently, there was no looking away. We could clearly hear the ancient, faint sound of crying rising up through their souls and in our hearts, so strong is it, that we haven't been able to put this to rest since

4

ALIEN 101: *THE DOWNLOAD*

Where to begin?

Things seemed to start off on the same note with Cafth too when he first started downloading on us. It almost seemed like he was teasing us along with riddles, as if he was trying to see if we could recall why he was in contact with us. We practically had to ask about everything, he did not seem to be there just to blurt things out. No, no, that would be too easy.

We had to know the right questions to ask, "ask and you shall receive," is a saying I understand fully now. That is exactly what we did, and that is exactly how we came to know some of the things myself and Amanda know now. I knew precisely where I wanted to start things off first with our new contact. I felt that I would need to understand some of the things in my personal life first before I would be able to come to an understanding of anything else. So I wanted to start in getting some insight into what comes my way and why, and the most recent incident came to mind was about a dream I'd just had.

Four days before Amanda had her encounter with the glitter-like being in her car, I had one of my grand "waking dreams." I call them that because these kinds of dreams are so real, it is really hard to believe it did not actually happen and there always is a paranormal element to them. I know that we have thousands of dreams a year and yet these particular kinds of dreams stick with me for a lifetime.

Why would I recall dreams of this sort if they truly were just another dream as any other? Personally, I would say this happens because these dreams really do count for something. Usually I feel as if I am being taught something (which I consider to be a part of my night schooling), tested on something or shown different possible outcomes life decisions can bring.

Well this one particular and recent dream I had, started off with me being in Orlando, Florida on a trip with a bunch of my friends, including Amanda. Amanda's family did live in Florida at the time, and we were actually planning a trip to do with a group of friends to go there. But instead of Amanda's parents being in my dream, my father was there in their place. That was odd in itself and I would later find it to be significant for him to be there also, because I later bumped into him a few times aboard UFO craft (nothing that he recalls personally).

In the dream, Amanda and my other friend, Olga, had stepped outside for a moment when I suddenly heard them call out to me. I went outside to see what was the matter and they pointed up to the sky where I saw the moon quickly darkening. It was daylight in the dream, but you could still clearly see the moon and it started shading in as if an eclipse was taking place.

As the moon became totally engulfed in darkness, suddenly an orangish-red, oblong, glowing object appeared in front of the darkened moon and it appeared to begin pulling it. I remember my friends referring to the orange object as maybe being the Hale-Bopp comet, since this dream did take place during that time, but I told them that was no comet.

The glowing object continued to drag the moon at an angle that made it almost seem like it was going to hit the Earth, but I had the notion in mind that maybe the angle of the horizon only made it seem that way. Nonetheless, as soon as the moon was out of sight there was a sudden "whooshing" of air as if something popped the Earth's protective bubble. The wind was so strong that houses began to blow down the street. My friends and I ran back into the house. Amanda and Olga ran to the basement and beckoned me to come down too, but I was determined to get my dad first who was snoozing in the next room.

Although I tried my heart out I couldn't physically make it to his room because the house was rocking so badly, so I tried yelling for him. I couldn't even hear my own voice leaving my lips, due to the loud roaring of the wind outdoors. I got out only a few cries for my father when it all suddenly ended, there was no more wind!

"It's over?" I remember saying to myself.

My dad then came out of the room towards me to see what I was making such a big fuss over. I was a bit overwhelmed and just motioned to him to give me a moment, when I heard the voices of people outside the front door.

I then went to the door to see if all of the people outside were okay and one man said, "Yeah we're alright, but it's dark outside!"

When that man said that it was as if I immediately knew that I would have to see these people through this change in our way of living, but it would take all our efforts together. I also remember thinking that we still did have electricity and other things of the sort to make survival easier. It then all ended there, the dream that is.

I can say, waking up after having a vivid and lucid experience like that can leave you searching out your room a bit to convince yourself that none of it really happened. I have had many dreams of this capacity before, but it's not like I have them on a regular basis where I can recall the whole thing. But when they come, they can pack a punch. Now I've come to accept these dreams as sort of a treat since it can be rare when I'm able to recall the whole view.

It is also quite common for experiencers of the alien and UFO phenomenon to be given different dream scenarios about the end of modern living. It seems that people are being observed as to how they will respond to a natural or un-natural disaster. I know in my scenarios that if I don't respond smartly, I'm given pointers at another time and a similar scenario is given until I feel I've reacted best. The reactions that I've felt best about are when I remain calm, think logically with my resources, and to look to work with others equally and not stand alone.

So four days later when Cafth came into the picture and offered himself as a guide into the unknown, I thought it would be neat to hear his insights on this latest dream of mine that I knew had alien hands in it. Amanda also had a recent dream of her own that she wanted him to analyze for her too.

This waking dream of hers happened to be the first that she had ever had of this kind, and it just so happened that she had this dream of hers the day after my dream. It seemed that we were being groomed to meet Cafth all that week, the timing was just too close to discount.

Amanda's dream occurred after she had laid down to take a nap that following afternoon. She went on to explain, "I suddenly found myself in the middle of ruins, all the buildings were literally flattened! But I knew it was near downtown Milwaukee, near Lake Michigan where we lived. I remember looking at the lake and wondering why the lake was a rustic-red color when a voice spoke up in my head and said, "The water reflects the color of the sky."

"Personally, I didn't know that. But sure enough when I looked up the sky was red! As I stood there I began to hear a woman screaming out, because someone she loved was lying dead in her arms. That's when I saw some men walking towards me, wearing some white protective suits. I saw one of them motion to the others to go and get me and I knew that wasn't a good idea, so I took off running."

"I remember though, that I couldn't run too well because the air was so polluted it was impossible to outrun them. I don't remember them catching me because I think I passed out or something. Then the next thing I know I'm in this like dentist chair surrounded by three men in gray pants, white shirts and blue ties. It seemed that they were examining me to see how it was that I survived, while others could not. I recall feeling horrible pain going down from my left shoulder down my side, and then the dream ended."

When Amanda awoke she claimed that the same pain going down from her shoulder still remained and it took some time for it to go away. When it finally did, she decided to go to her computer to type up what she remembered so she wouldn't forget the details. As she wrote down her dream, oddly enough, a voice popped in her head and reminded her about an incident that happened to her about a year earlier. Of course having that voice come forward was startling to her, but the amazement of the slight pointer it gave, stunned her even more.

Amanda had a brand new pair of boots that she had only wore a few times before, and one day when she went to go wear them she found them full of mud way past the ankle part.

I remember her saying, "Heidi did you wear my boots or something?"

I couldn't make any sense of her accusation since I am two sizes bigger than she is, so I think I said something to the effect of, "Are you crazy woman? How could I?"

We never could make sense of how it is that she got mud that high on her boots and of that color, a rustic-red. Well, that voice that occurred to her told her that she was wearing those boots when that incident, her dream, happened! That explained that mystery of the muddied boots, but it just added another one! How in the heck could she have mud on her boots from a **dream**, so to speak?! We needed some answers for sure, because we could not make any sense out her dream, nor my own.

We thought about our dreams independently, because at the time Amanda was still not too hip to the ideas of UFO's and other phenomena yet. Then of course three days later, in pops this glittering creature in Amanda's car, then Cafth, and you all now know the story.

So I asked Cafth, "What was the deal with Amanda's boots getting all muddied up? She doesn't remember actually being amongst blasted down buildings, in fact, she could not have been since all these buildings are still standing."

Cafth began, "You will be the ones to destroy yourselves, and we showed her what it may look like."

"So she was there as if it happened?" I asked.

"I am not in charge of dreams, so I cannot say."

I've learned that when he says he can't say something he will ignore any further requests on the topic. But in this instance I didn't know this about Cafth, so I pursued.

"Yeah, but you said to us before, that you know all that we do daily, so can't you say if she was or was not there? Was it really a part of our future she was taken to?"

Cafth uttered in a jokingly manner, "Do you want to get me in trouble? I can't say and it is not beneficial for you to know."

Cafth had explained to us earlier that he had access to some crystals that had souls in them. That these crystal souls recorded the lives and activities of individuals. He was also clear to state that none of the crystals on Earth were like his crystals, but people like to give crystals quality as if they were.

So with these crystals, all Cafth had to do was hold our life crystals to see what it is we have experienced or done at anytime. So I knew he could answer my question. But, I was just learning that he was also obligated to keep some things under wrap, where he could not speak on some issues.

Being an adamant Star Trek fan, I could not help but to think that they have a Holo-deck, or something that they used to give these waking dream experiences. For those of you who don't know what that is, they are hologram programs used to entertain or do whatever you like. The program's holograms are very much solid where one can actually interact with the environment being presented, only if you are an actor on Star Trek of course.

Since I ran into a brick wall with that line of questioning with Cafth, I left that topic alone and went on to ask about my dream. Once again he stated that he did not do dreams, but I told him about it anyway.

He said, "Yes I know the dream and I will tell you this much…"

I remember thinking, "Alright, I broke through, he's going to tell me all I need to hear, whoopee!"

Cafth began, "The moon turned dark because the darkness in the Earth was pulling it towards the Earth."

"Okay," I said waiting in anticipation to see what the heck that meant and what else there was to be said about the whole thing. But there was silence, I've also learned that at times I have to keep Cafth and Soforus going in their thoughts. It seems that they either forget that we cannot read their minds or they assume that we know what they mean even if they just sputter out a few words.

So I continued to question him, "Okay so the moon got dark, but then it started to move and soon after, I saw what looked like a ship dragging it. What does that all mean?"

"Well, we saw what was happening and so we removed the moon." Cafth said briefly.

Like I said, they swear that we would understand what all of this meant, so I begged for more info and he said, "The Shadows did this in your dream and they may do so soon."

"The Shadows?" I asked emphatically.

"Yes, you have called them the Shadow People in the past."

"What, you mean those nosey, shadowy looking things I've seen for years hanging around me? So what, they are as negative as I have felt of them, they are real?" I was just astonished with him mentioning these Shadow People.

"Yes, they are very real."

For some reason, I just knew that the whole purpose between us and their mission was about to be unfolded. I had this sinking feeling in the pit of stomach, and I almost didn't want to press on. I had dealt with this presence of Shadow People for some time, but I did not know how to address them. I had only heard of a few people ever speak of this presence, and each time I heard of the conversation, I was the one to initiate it.

Even before Bob was put under hypnosis for what happened on our Arkansas trip and spoke about the Shadow People, I had first asserted my concern about their presence surrounding me. Sometimes I just like to hear something totally spontaneous from someone. That way I know for sure that what they say is authentic and not have the possibility of being predetermined because it had been mentioned before.

"Then again," I thought to myself, as Amanda was still in the middle of channeling Cafth, "what Bob had to say about the Shadow People feels a lot like what Cafth is getting at and I have never mentioned this to Bob."

So I opened up the floor to hear Cafth out and I pushed on, "You mean like what Bob had said about the Shadow People coming after me to stop me from completing my mission, that's all true?"

"Yes."

"Like in killing me or something?" I just wanted to be clear on that point, I'm sure anyone could understand that!

"Yes. But that is not the only way they could stop you."

"Go on." I said intently.

"They could also drive you to lose control of who you are, or influence you to go a negative way."

Then I recalled the part in Bob's hypnosis where he described being shown what the Shadow People would do to him if they got to him or me. Then the beings proceeded to disconnect his emotions from something he had resolved. In his case it was the grief and sorrow he felt, when his twin sister was killed. Just as he was describing what they were going to do, Bob screamed out in terror, unable to control what he was feeling. Several moments later, he was put at ease and went on to say that they put his emotions back in place.

He then said, "I believe you, I believe you. They wanted to prove to me that it can be done, and they did it!"

So in reflecting back to what Cafth was telling me, well, it was hard to be skeptical as to the capabilities of these Shadow People doing this. But why bother with me? I wasn't anybody, okay so Cafth said I was his family. But besides that, I still had a goal with no target in mind. How was I to be such a big threat? Plus now I had Amanda on my side who was also there to join forces to set the record straight about alien stuff that we really didn't even know about. Lovely just lovely, then add some dark character on our tail, that really added to the mood of all this.

Well, we were in for a treat alright, Alien 101 through 201, I presume. Because Cafth was about to do an intro course and a run down on all this Shadow People business with great agility and speed. I could only hope and pray that I could keep up with these new truths being bestowed upon me.

5

ALIEN 201: *THE ADVANCED COURSE*

Puzzled and intensely curious, I listened closely to what Cafth had to say about "The Shadows," as he called them. He went on to explain that these Shadows were all the horrible things we could ever think of. Put all that negativity in one heap, and that would be the beloved Shadow People.

"Cafth," I said quietly, "are you trying to tell me that there is such a thing as the devil?"

I couldn't help but to make the relation, it sounded a lot like it to me: Something dark, shapeless, and horrible…what else could it be but a devil or something like it?!

Cafth found it humorous that I would relate the name but he said, "Essentially, yes, but that is a human term for what and who the Shadows are."

Whoa! Now I had a hard time swallowing that one, because I for one am not a religious person. But I am very spiritual, and I had wiped out all thought of there being a hoofed man running around in our midst. I did not believe that there could ever be such an entity that was so horrible and allowed to exist by our creator. That is, besides man, people can be pretty mean and nasty.

Cafth then interrupted my thoughts, as if he were listening, and said, "Whether you believe it or not, they do exist and you need to be aware of them."

I had to be honest with myself though, that the concept of such a thing had to exist somehow in some form. I always wondered about how the idea of a negative entity has lasted so long. I mean even a rumor dies out at some point, but here we are thousands of years later and there is still "devil talk."

Ugh, I hate the thought of it. Even the name is disturbing for me to hear since I had blocked and resisted my senses to even let that name through. It takes me back to the pews in church I sat in as a child, thinking all this stuff was a bunch of baloney with that devil stuff.

I explained to Cafth how people envision the devil through artist renditions of a multi-specied creature, half man and half animal. So I was curious then about how this thing truly appears to be. All I had ever seen personally was a large massive shadowy looking being, so I did not feel certain if I was seeing it for what it was.

"They can take any form." Cafth asserted.

"That's the same concept the Bible has about the devil, that you never know what form the devil will take," I said emphatically to Cafth as if I was schooling him on the Bible.

Cafth then maneuvers Amanda's mouth to form an awkward smile, "Yes, I do know that. Who do you think helped influence what was to be written in the Bible? We have been around for a long time. We are in constant contact with The Source on how to guide us to help others."

Now, he was getting really, really deep and I was just exploding with a billion questions. "Aliens have ties in the content of the Bible?" I thought.

I know that what moved people to write what they did in the Bible all came from or worked with the same source. These beings that I'm speaking of also worked for the same source, so it made sense to me then. In fact, my own realization and recollections of The Source are my main drive as well. But encouragement by these non-human beings helped build on that inspiration to delve more and write this book, in fact.

I had always suspected that the Bible had alien helping hands, I mean even the basic stuff, like with those three wise men following "a star." Come on, it doesn't take a genius to figure out that stars don't move and wait for you to catch up. Then there's Ezekiel's Wheel, sounded like a modern day UFO description practically. I was about to start asking more about that topic, but I really wanted to finish off what I had started with the Shadows. Then suddenly, another perturbing thought came into mind.

"Hold on. I know a lot of people that claim to have seen owls, deer, even lions in their bedroom that they relate to as being some kind of alien abduction experience. Even I have had beings come to me in different forms, ones I really did not care for either. I have seen them as a clown, and several times now as something I really cannot stand, spiders! Big ones, the size of me and they scare the crap out of me! So you're saying that all those ones that take on another form are these bad Shadow guys?!"

Cafth answered again, "We do not change form. Forms are changed to deceive, so you cannot see what they truly are. What other purpose would it serve?"

"Well I thought at first that other forms were taken so they would not scare people so badly. You know, so they appear as something we can relate to and accept. I thought they were doing people a favor. I mean, it would be a lot easier for me to think and relate to others that I was confronted by a man eating spider than an alien! Then I'd be able to dismiss it all as a dream or waking dream, I suppose."

But when I think on it, I really had no good feelings about seeing a 4 foot spider in my bedroom with rows of eyes that went on forever! It would really make me distraught when I or a roommate would find me scrambling in my apartment to find a shoe, screaming that a giant spider was just there! Thinking if only I could kill that dang thing then it would never come back.

I know it sounds funny and all, but boy is that a horrible feeling. It's like something from a horror movie just stepped out of the screen and into reality and it ain't pretty at any angle. What do you do in that situation, really? Run, hide, scream?

You really feel like a bug caught in a spider's web and you are about to be feasted upon. You look into their eyes and you are just paralyzed with fear. I've been lucky to not have been completely frozen though, because

I've always been able to react to their presence and go looking for a shoe or something to smack them with.

I have not stopped to research the topic on what others may have felt in their encounters with beings that present themselves as being something familiar, so I cannot speak for all. But in speaking from my perspective, how could a being that invokes fear and control on another with just a glare, have completely good intentions?

I have met several people who have spoken to me about their experiences though, and I do know that those that speak about seeing animals and what not, say that it is the eyes of these animals that are so compelling. Compelling to the point that their eyes have them under their control where they cannot move and fear pumps throughout their souls, while in these being's presence. Doesn't sound **good** to me.

I know that I never found it thrilling being near those kinds of being's, but I know the argument that some of these abductees feel enriched after these and other encounters. That some feel that they are being primed for something wonderful that's soon to happen. It is almost as if they feel that they are a part of something that is essentially benefitting to them and others, no matter how much pain they are put through by these beings. I can see how having that thought of being helpful may make some abductees feel useful and go along with what's being done to them too though.

I don't want to blast anyone for what they believe to be real for them. But I do want to show a logical and true reason as to what is really going on with these beings that disguise themselves under the hide of an animal.

Soon after Cafth's statement, the thought occurred to me of how people encounter beings. Sometimes, the person experiences missing time that they have no recollection about. Then they pop up later wondering what happened to the time, and may or may not have odd markings on their bodies and a suspicion that something unearthly happened to them.

The most famous beings that everyone has heard of or seen, is the gray colored alien with the big, black eyes. Then in the media all you hear about is how they slice, dice and extract specimens from innocent people that are rendered paralyzed, but who would rather be kicking and scream-ing the whole while. That sounds pleasant enough, but then they practi-cally forget the whole thing unless put under hypnosis or have flashes of memory come forward.

Well I used to think, if these beings were really cruel, they would leave the person with their memory fully intact. That way they would remem-ber the entire horrible ordeal and would be more likely to show signs of Post Traumatic Stress Disorder (PTSD). I actually thought that was an act of mercy on their part to take the memory away.

I also expressed this idea to Cafth and he told me, through Amanda of course, that, "This is another form of hiding that some of them do."

"Yes, but they didn't change form and a lot of people express how they really learn a lot from these beings. In fact, you say that I go back to your ship three times a week and I don't remember everything." I spoke up to Cafth.

"**Most** of the Grays are under the influence of the Shadows (all of the abducting Grays). But not all Grays are bad (the non-abducting Grays), it is a shame that they all have to live with a bad reputation," Cafth responded.

Cafth then paused, showing that he truly felt bad for the Grays that had not been a part of the Shadow's actions.

"We have different reasons for our actions. We do not let you remem-ber things for your own protection and ours. They do not let you remem-ber to hide their true purposes," Cafth ensured.

I was deeply interested to hear more about the Grays involvement with the Shadows, so I pressed on, "The Grays are connected with the Shadows? But, so many, heck most people claim to have contact with the Grays, and they're working with who you consider the bad guys?"

"This is of concern," Cafth expressed as if it was part of his agenda.

"Whoa, this doesn't sound too good. All these people that talk about them…!"

I really started to show concern myself about this matter, there were so many people talking about the Grays this, the Grays that, and here they nce of something equivalent to the devil. Oh this was

All the experiments performed on people, including the cutting and giving birth to hybrid, human-alien babies, what's it all mean? My mind was just jumbled with speculations and possibilities. So I asked Cafth what was going on with these Grays and Shadows who were working on human bodies all the time?

"The experiments are being done to develop a new kind of being that can live upon the Earth."

"Okay, so you mean they want to be able to live amongst us and the only way they can do so is by using some of our own biological information or something?" I asked sincerely.

"No, this new being is something they want to inhabit the Earth. Their plan is to have the hybrids be the main occupants of Earth, with the assistance of some of those people that they take to breed them. These beings and humans will all be under the influence of the Shadows, the Shadows will then be the only inhabitants of Earth."

That went way over my head, but I understood it alright. There's been lots of talk about how humans are losing their abilities to reproduce, and that it's apparent in the amount of sperm count in men today. That this has been a concern for Gray alien beings and so they were creating a hybrid race so that we may live on. Then there's also been the talk of the Grays dying off and losing their planet, and needing a means to reproduce and a place to live. So I tended to think along those lines as to why they were creating this hybrid race, but it seems I was wrong. Once we're all said and done, in comes the *supposed* underdog to take over things and people helped them along.

I began inquiring, "But some of the people that are being taken for these experiments can recall volunteering or agreeing to the role that they play in all this. How can it be that they would want something like that happening to them? I would think not."

Cafth responded to these questions by saying, "Many people are under the influence of the Shadows also, and they have rendered their dedication and allegiance to the other Source. The Dark Source. They take on certain roles to help continue the Shadow's plans, as in helping to abduct more people and reassure the other victims that all is well that it being done to them."

"Are people aware of this and to whom they are pledging their loyalties with? I mean you're saying that they can take on different forms, and that doesn't sound fair that they are fooling people to believe they are something different than they are!" I went on.

"Humans are born with knowing the difference between what is right and what is wrong. It is when they welcome to listen to what is wrong, that is when they also welcome in the darkness. Some do this while in this life, others are of alien descent also and have volunteered to have this done to them while in this life and form. The Shadows are very cruel and do not spare even their own kind to their horrors."

Cafth continued on, "Some of the people that have these experiences, are just simply venerable. If you are strong in your convictions of doing what is right, the Shadows cannot influence you."

"Everyone has their moments of weakness though, I don't care who it is, and what of kids that have abduction experiences happen to them?" I had be sure I was asking all I could on this.

"Too many questions at once," Cafth spurted out in a confused manner, then Amanda's face scrunched all up.

I suppose I get carried away at times, it's just having all this access can really get you rolling with questions. I apologized and asked him to go ahead and take one at a time and I promised I would try to pace myself better.

Cafth then seemed to gather himself and began again, "In answering your first question, "Yes, but one must keep up their energy level to not fall victim to the Shadows. And for your second inquiry: Humans have a thing called "innocence" that makes them unaccountable for their actions, but now even that barrier is being crossed. This highly concerns us."

"I don't think I'm understanding you completely. You're saying that these Shadows are not the greatest people, but what's so wrong in their ways. For the most part, they really are doing experiments on those who let them, and they're going to make use of a planet that people will inevitably destroy." I was doing my best to rationalize away the reasons behind the Shadow's actions.

"Do you still not see who the Shadows are?" I suppose he got a bit perturbed by my comment. "There are people being tortured or influenced blindly."

"Hold on," I thought to myself, "no one ever said anything about being tortured!"

I know the abduction experience is not always one of pleasure, but I never outright thought of it as being torture!

I felt like there was a lot more that Cafth wanted to say about all this and I was ready to go on for as long as it would take for me to grasp everything. I really had a lot of questions to pursue with him. Then break down those questions into even smaller, more detailed questions just to make sure it would all sink in. There was so much to learn and I could have gone on forever, but Cafth will interrupt me at times to let me know that poor Amanda gets exhausted from their hook-up.

I get so involved with what is being discussed at times and in seeing in my mind's eye, the vision of Cafth, that I often forget that my dear friend is laying there extending herself to the extreme. So I had to let things go for then and let Amanda come forward so we could discuss the juicy tidbits fed to us in that session. Usually when Amanda awakens, her eyes hurt her so badly that she is unable to focus well, nor stand a light to be on for a good 15 minutes.

But then after she comes around, we'll sit around and talk about all that was said and if she got any extra insight from her angle. Generally, she can feel what Cafth is feeling as he is talking and get the full intention of what he means. So I like to get the extra scoop on it all if I can, so it's always brought up to see what his perspective was at the time.

We had a lot to discuss after this session, a lot that we still did not understand. It's a good thing that we had an easily accessible instructor that we knew we could speak to again to clear up our confusion, whenever Amanda felt up to it of course. But she would conjure up the energy she needed pretty regularly so we could both continue to indulge into the highly unusual circumstances Cafth was explaining to us. There was still so much that needed to be told.

6

THE ODDS: *2 OUT OF 3*

For the next couple of days, Amanda and I discussed our latest expedition into our world, through alien eyes.

Amanda said she felt Cafth was filled with great concern for our safety, as if we were almost in some immediate danger of some kind. She also said that she was deeply aware that Cafth had only dumped a fraction of what he had intended. She knew that we had only begun and felt the dire need to continue on in our discussions with him. So we decided to put together our thoughts and questions and strike up conversation with him again later that same evening.

Just before we speak to Cafth, usually we will sit and write down all that we intend to ask him, which I found to be quite useful too. Because a lot of the time I will become so involved in one conversation with Cafth, that I would forget all the other questions I had on my mind then too. But sometimes it really is beneficial for me to just carry on in one topic though. Then other times I could just kick myself for forgetting something that had been bugging me to ask him about. That then means I would have to wait for the next time Amanda was able to find the time, and mainly the energy to talk to him.

Both of us were full-time college students at the time and worked, so you can imagine how hectic it could be for both of us to get a chance to speak with Cafth. I have to admit, in the beginning this was not as much of a problem though. We still had the "awe factor" going on where we were just amazed that we were having the contact that we were. We were still shook up with the sudden channeling thing and the words of wisdom from an unknown origin pouring through. So we really were just going at it with all our might for a month or so in the beginning.

Just as a note on this though, there was no way we could ever get bored in having this kind of contact. But as time passed, we began to dwindle down in our contact time when we kept running into blocked responses. It was like Cafth had said all he was allowed for us to do our mission and the rest was off limits and up to us to find out. We understood that, and later just had sessions where we would try to clarify our memory on something he had said before.

Even then he would say, "I have told you that information already."

He wasn't being testy, I just think he did not completely understand the limits of human memory or something. But he would repeat his messages for us still, with an added note for us to seek answers within ourselves.

It would have been easier if he had allowed us to tape our sessions though, but he said this was for our ears only and that it could possibly fall into the wrong hands. So I am replaying this whole book from mostly mine and some of Amanda's memory and minor notes I took here and there. But I should state that Amanda's memory does not always serve her very well when she is in her meditative state, so I've had to rely on most of the information from my own recollections.

I could not even save this book on my computer while typing it up because Cafth said the government could look at my files without me even having a phone modem hook-up, and with my computer turned off even! They really must have gotten their hands on some neat technology to do that kind of stuff. Technology I'm certain was borrowed.

But I must say I am accurate with the accounts shared here, since most of this is pretty darn unforgettable. My biggest concern is that my words are fluent here without much error because this book was also not to be read by anyone else until its publication. So all of the contents you read here are edited by none other than myself, over the past few years.

But I did begin writing this book only a few months after the encounters with Cafth began, and as time has passed I've grown and recalled much more than what I could even fit here in this one book now. But what's most important is what's being presented here, and the very human journey I took to getting to my understandings and I hope that perspective makes it easier for others to relate to.

Well, when we finally got back to talking to Cafth I started right up from where we left off about the Shadows and the torture thing that he had mentioned before.

"What kind of torturing are we talking about here? Are you speaking about the way they abduct people and perform experiments on them?" I began.

"Yes, that is a form of what I mean. But it goes much further than that." Cafth started off saying quietly.

"The Shadows are enslaving humans just as they do the Gray beings."

"How so?" I asked.

"Once you welcome these beings into your life, you are a part of them and work for them. They control you and influence you in your choices throughout your days and life, and they are not a positive influence."

Once again I had to think of the imagery that was taught to me in Sunday school class. I was told that there is an angel on your right shoulder and a devil on your left, fighting to tell you what to do. So I made mention of this to Cafth to see if this is relative to what he was saying.

Cafth answered, "Essentially yes, there is a battle going on with that."

"Then if that is true, then that proves also that if a person is being influenced by these Shadows, that person is not all bad either. I mean, we all have a dark side. So these people can pull themselves out from under this control thing you're talking about then, right?"

"Yes, but they cannot be loyal to both sources. If that is the case, they will still be under the influence of the Shadows to some extent. Any amount of their influence is not a good thing."

"I see. Huh…so these things just like to do this to make sure we make the wrong decisions in our life? I could never really quite understand the whole concept of a devil-like deity, going around doing rotten things just for the mere pleasure of saying they had the control."

"Not just control, power is what they are truly after," Cafth said.

"Power. But why?"

"That is just what they do and seek. This is not the first planet they have done this to, but I cannot speak further on that topic. It is truly a sad thing."

I got a little clearer on some of the general ideas and agenda of these Shadow beings, and I decided it was time to nitpick a bit at some specifics.

So I asked, "Could you elaborate on some details about the Shadows, like where they live on Earth since earlier you implied that this is their home too?"

Cafth paused briefly as if to think about whether or not he was allowed to say, then said, "In the center of your planet."

Whoa, that response reminded me about something I read somewhere once. I used to read a lot on any topic of the un-ordinary to let myself know there were stranger things out there than my life. It really did help me out.

I read, starting back in the times of Assyro-Babylonian King Gilgamesh, there was a speculation of there being inhabitants on the interior of our world. This notion became modernized with the addition of Edmond Halley's findings, the same Halley that predicted and discovered the showing of the Halley comet.

Halley found that the magnetic north was not always in the same place and it's changes could be predicted. The only way Halley could explain this phenomena away was to speculate that Earth was a twin, that meant that the Earth had an outer shell with an inner nucleus. He then suggested that they both had their own separate axis, and magnetic poles to do what his findings were showing.

For Halley to prove his theories back then in the 17th century was quite a feat in itself. The Christian faith was undoubtedly the predominant force when it came to other-worldly thinking, that there was nothing in the center of Earth but Hell. I thought that Christian idea of where Hell is, was interesting too.

e in this day and age with all of our technology to look most anywhere we want on and around our planet and we still referred to Hell as being below the Earth's surface. What a coincidence that I am hearing from an alien, that some sinister beings reside below our surface too. I got a kick out of the way Halley backed himself up in his convictions though. He explained to people that since God had stocked up the Earth's surface with life, he would most certainly would have done the same with the inner world.

Makes sense to me now, but I wonder if it was God related fully. It only took an alien to tell me directly, but at least I understood it at some point in my life. I was eager to learn more from Cafth on this inner world commotion. So I asked him to continue on in explaining this place.

"The inside of your planet is very much like the shape of the human body, but it is a place of misery."

"What is so awful about this place?" I asked.

"Darkness lives there and they torture their enslaved there. Their physical and spiritual bodies (humans and other enslaved aliens) are put through terrible things for mere pleasure. They are even eaten alive by the Shadows or their pet creatures just to inflict pain and show who's in control. A soul can be made to feel the same pain, if not more than the physical, but last longer in duration."

Once again, I couldn't help but to think about references to the Bible and the imagery of Hell. I was truly still having a hard time accepting that there was something as horrible as demon-like creatures and now Hell too?! This was all way too much, how could this be that an alien entity speaking through my friend was schooling me on so many excerpts from the Bible? I had tossed so much of that out of my mind for years now and here it was staring me in the face again, this time with big-black eyes.

I would often catch myself testing Amanda just to see if she was still just trying to mess with me with all this alien channeling thing. I know it sounds stupid, but even with all I have seen and known to be true, it still gets hard to trust your senses. I cannot help but to be my worst critic, and

I think I do that every once and awhile just to try to make my life simpler, if not for at least a few moments. A few moments is all it lasts too, because my knowledge is too strong to even let me try to fool myself.

So of course I had to make mention to Cafth that this all sounded like Religion 101 to me again, like straight out of the Bible. Then before he even answered me via Amanda, I got the answer personally in my head, "Who do you think helped inspire the Bible?" It was like a repeating echo from the previous conversation I had with Cafth, just resonating through my head.

You know, I think he knew what was going through my head too, because he never made the motion as if he was going to answer me. Besides that, he was probably too busy focusing on putting that echoing thought in my head in the first place, which was fine.

So with that answered and out of the way, I proceeded to go on to find out more about the torturing of the enslaved in this inner world.

Cafth continued to speak again, "Those that are there, let the Shadows influence them, not knowing what would be the end result."

"You mean that there are mainly regular people down there suffering at the hands of these Shadows?"

"Yes."

"How many are we talking about here?"

"Billions, 2 out of 3 will go to the Shadows."

"….2/3rds….2 out of 3…," I just kept repeating over and over aloud and in my head. How could this be? That's way too many.

I blurted out, "Something's got to stop this, that's crazy, those are horrible odds! What are they doing with them down there?"

Cafth knew I was upset by these revelations and understood that I was getting way ahead of myself and said, "We know the pain this must cause you to know. But imagine how we feel when we look down upon your planet and see this with our own eyes. Something is being done, this is why we are here and why we sent you two there."

"We're a part of the solution?" I pondered to myself.

"What can we do to help? This sounds like an ancient old battle going on, so what could we possibly do now that would help turn things around?"

I just couldn't understand what could little ol' me and Amanda do that would just foil such grand plans of doom!

As I sat there imagining what our role could be, Cafth interrupted again and said, "Others have been sent there as well, to do what we have sent you for. 715 from our ship alone have been sent, and 64 for your particular mission."

"Oh, well that's good then, are they getting things done?" I kind of fumbled along in saying this since I had no idea exactly what was to be done.

"Some are doing well, yet most are having problems dealing with their connection to us. They do not always seek to understand things fully and can drive themselves mad, ignore everything or some even kill themselves."

Cafth seemed dismayed and saddened that most do not make it. But he did go on to say, "I am very proud of the way you two are handling yourselves. You are very strong, keep up the good work."

I remarked, "Thanks, it sometimes has been tough for me personally to remain firm in my convictions on the subject at times. But I have always bounced back somehow."

Saying that, really took me back. I couldn't help but to flashback onto the time when I really came close to giving up on all of this UFO business after so many years of being alone on this odd voyage.

When I was living down in Iowa in the summer of 1990 in the small town of Keokuk, along with my friend Lisa and her family. Her family was highly religious and were constantly picking at me about following the UFO topic and studying too much on the devil-aliens. One night Lisa's family had really gotten to me with their comments and I stormed out behind their home into a large, vacant parking lot.

I stared up into the evening sky with an anger in my heart so strong. It was like an anger of betrayal. I felt as if I had been misled in following my instincts, which somehow led me to this negative and unacceptable thing in space. I still had a bit of religious upbringing in my blood, so the possibilities of following a negative entity was still very plausible and not something I was wanting in my life.

I asked strongly in my mind and muttered under my breath these words as I gazed up into that night sky, "If you have anything to do with the devil or anything like that, I am through with learning any more about you! So you had better show yourself now, or this is it!"

I meant every word of what I was saying. When I think about it now, I have no idea who or whom I was directing my demands to. I just knew that I needed some proof now that I was on the right path, or I was done with "them," whoever they were.

After muttering my words, I stared impatiently at the darkened night sky. Only a few moments passed when I saw what looked like a couple of shooting stars, including one that did zig-zags. But they were so high up there was no telling exactly what was doing these stunts, so I said, "That's not good enough!"

Boy did I have my nerve! But I was really in a desperate and venerable time, when I needed all the reassurance I could get. No sooner had I said those words aloud, did I get my response. A small, fully lit, saucer-shaped craft appeared at one end of the parking lot just above tree level. As soon as I caught a glimpse of it, it streaked across the entire length of the lot, lighting the whole thing up for a few moments!

I burst into tears with delight and wonder.

"They heard me," I said to myself as I continued to cry and shake in awe.

I felt such a love and comforting feeling from whomever brushed over me in that craft. I do not know how, but I knew that "they" were always near and that I could call on them anytime. I then promised them in my mind and heart that I would never doubt their reason of *being* again.

They had totally blown my socks off and nothing could ever knock my convictions again, I was also sure to let Lisa's family know that too. Lisa and her family saw the look in my eyes and knew that I was serious about what I had just experienced and not joking. But then the next morning they came up with some sorry story about a meteor shower that night. Nice save, but no dice.

I tuned in to all the weather and news broadcasts I could and never heard a mention of meteor showers, and I'd never heard of one fly so low and parallel to the ground and be saucer shaped. People are so quick to put down anything you come to grips with if they cannot relate. Well, that was just too bad. I got the answers I needed to regain my strength. You would think that strength would last a lifetime, but still I have teetered a bit here and there. But I have come out okay so far and that is what I feel counts the most.

I then turned my attention back to what Cafth was saying about the 715 beings sent from his ship.

"What happens when these other 713 beings that you have sent down here, come back to the ship and they weren't successful in doing their mission? Do you guys like put them down for it or anything?"

You know I was really asking for myself, just in case I did not live up to my end of the bargain whatever that might be.

"No they are not punished, they are taught more lessons. But sometimes they do not return," Cafth said.

I remembered Cafth had said this about one of my sisters, that I knew to also be of a different origin. He told me that she had strayed too far and may not be able to return home because of it. I remembered he mentioned how truly sad he was about it, but it was up to her to change that fate and said she would be missed dearly if she didn't. I have since been trying to wake my sister up to this subject so she won't, unknowingly, detach herself from who she really is. But still that is not exactly my place, so I try to only offer to help when asked.

"So there are others here at work to do the same thing we are here to do and that is to…in your distinct words…?" I was really reaching here.

"Tell people about the reasons of our presence."

The *reasons*? Heck I could write a book just listing my speculations of the reasons from what he has told me already!

He went on, "People must understand who we are and why we are here. Be sure to tell them, that is important."

"Okay, sure."

This was the first time he had outright dictated something to me as if it were absolutely dire to know. He did not need to worry, he had my full attention for whatever he had to say. I suppose it was then that I began to understand the legwork that Cafth was meaning for us to do. Certain things had to be let out and be made known to the public. It seemed there was only one sure way to do this, I had to write a book, I suppose.

7

SPEAKING OUT: *FINDING THE COURAGE*

A book, that would make sense for me to do one. I especially got the idea to do one after Cafth said something like, "Your book will turn out nicely." A nice little subtle hint he gave out to me right after I asked how we were to let people know about their agenda for being here, since we were told not to speak on it.

Even after he had said this about a book, I really just wanted to start up a new UFO group. I always knew I had a book in me, but I still didn't feel much like a writer. But I was a sociable person and thought a group was the best way to go to share and relate some experiences with others. I had always felt comfortable attending the groups I was involved with in the past, so I figured others would be too. But my timing never seemed to be right to put a group together for a long time.

My life was full already, so I didn't think it would be fair to start something that I could not dedicate the proper attention to. It wasn't until a little over a year after meeting Cafth, in July of 1998, that I started a group called UFO2U. Amanda suggested I use that name since it was my screen name on the web at one time (but no longer) and I was stumped on what name to give it.

At the time that I started this group I still didn't feel that I could be totally open about all that I knew on the UFO subject. I wanted to be able to be done with this book so I would be free to speak on it's contents. But by the way I was driven to spontaneously start this group, I found that it didn't matter about just me and where I stood. It was all about creating the opportunity for people to meet and share, and that is exactly how UFO2U has turned out to be.

I started this group also because the groups I had been involved with in the past seemed to be somewhat limiting in one sense or another. There was always some kind of path each group went down. There were the groups where you either had to be an experiencer of UFO phenomenon or posses a good attention span so you would be able to sit through a few hours of informative lecturing on the UFO subject.

Both types of groups were good though, and served their purpose for me at the times when I needed them. But I was certain it would be more thought provoking to have a group where anyone who was an experiencer or simply had a curiosity about the subject, could just stop in to discuss or lend an ear to the conversation at hand. I wanted people to just get involved and be made aware of what is out there and have the opportunity to question some of the people who claim to have "been there and done that."

To me, that was the whole purpose of having a group based on UFO's. I felt I needed to get to the everyday people and not limit it. What good is it to sit on the kind of information some contactees, such as myself and Amanda are receiving and just hoard it?! What good does that do? Enlighten us? Yes, indeed it would. And there we would sit, just full of **it** and ourselves, thinking we were better than everyone else. We would no doubt, be alone in that thought too.

It was thoughts like this that also convinced me, way before this Cafth thing started, to start speaking out about my experiences. Myself and my friend Bonnie, were asked to be a part of a panel to discuss our experiences at a huge science fiction and gaming convention held here in Milwaukee. I love these kinds of conventions, not only because I'm an avid science fiction lover, but because they also allow for topics such as UFO's to be included in their line-up.

This was my first time I was to speak out to the public on the topic, and this sci-fi convention was no little event either. Before I really knew what I had gotten myself into, I agreed to be a part of the panel. I of course felt honored to have been one of the few from the M.A.S.E. group to have been asked. I suppose Bonnie and I were a bit more outspoken than most, go figure. But I really had quite a deep set fear of speaking in public, and I went to extreme measures to try and overcome this in about a month before the panel was to take place.

The measures I took and the results I got to overcome this fear is a book in itself, to be brief, they did not work. But somehow I managed to get through the talk. In fact I really got the ball rolling, which surprised myself and others on the panel that knew of my fear. One of the members of the panel happened to be a renowned researcher and author on the topic of UFO's. After the panel, the researcher was impressed with the comments I made during the discussion. So afterwards, he came to ask me if I would join him on another panel he was going to be on later that same day. I was of course shocked, but agreed to join him.

It was kind of funny how I managed on that panel since it was made up of scientists and researchers, all discussing the scientific details of alien technology. Then there I was. I sat there listening to all the nuts and bolts of how they suspected alien crafts worked and all. Then I would kind of straighten up in my seat and blink a few times and just try to break things down to the audience in plain English. To say the least, it was an experience and I really enjoyed it.

It really felt good to present to people a face they could place some of the UFO stories and speculations to. I think most of the people that sat through those panels really appreciated the human interaction element and first hand details. Because afterwards a lot of the people came up to me to discuss some topics a little further on the things I mentioned and not so much of the researchers.

"People really want to learn more about this." I thought to myself. "Someway, somehow, I'd like to do more of these talks."

Well later, I did get my wish and got to do a few more panels here and there. Doing those panels was just something that I felt I needed to do way before my lessons from Cafth. But now with Cafth's connection, the urge grew even more so to expand my horizons. At times I've felt as if I was just going to burst from the seams to tell people about some of the extraordinary events that I have witnessed with Amanda.

Earlier I mentioned how Cafth suggested us to be careful about the information he was telling us. He basically said that the real crucial bits were for our ears only until I would put this all in writing and out in hard copy. Once that would be done then it would, more-or-less, be safe for us to talk freely on the subject. The crucial bits are the parts he told us about the Shadows and some of their agendas. So most of what I am speaking of in these pages was totally off limits for us to discuss for a long time and I found this really difficult.

I really did understand why he placed restrictions on this information, especially when he said it could be a threat to our well-being. He said there are some people who may catch word of our info and want it to end with us or slow it's dispersal down. So by having a book written and out, it would be a tad bit too late for anyone to stop us from letting out this information. But, this was some heavy stuff he was laying out to us and I really thought it to be important for people to know what was going on as soon as possible. But I suppose there is a time and a place for everything and I trusted when he said I'd know when the time was ripe for this book to be released.

So here I am writing all that I know down. Sometimes I don't know what I am going to focus on next, but I just let it flow to lead me to wherever it should. If there was a point to be made at this moment if I were speaking out to an audience of people, I would make mention how the first step has already been taken in the right direction because even to listen shows a person cares to know.

I truly understand that it's difficult to let some of the wild theories and research out there to enter your mind as a possible truth to things on the whole alien phenomenon. But to even consider what's being presented here, if people only knew the magnitude of what that means.

If there was anything that I have learned through my lifelong interactions with people, is that they just are not concerned enough about the right things. You can't make people care about anything if they don't want to, but I know it's one of my goals to at least put out the information just in case someone finds the need to know. One good example of lacks of interest, is in our planet Earth, without it you are nowhere. How could we dare ignore all that is going on with this planet?

When I sit and listen to Cafth, I feel such a somberness in his voice that tears at my heart when he speaks about the shape the Earth is in. He just does not understand our neglects. Then when I stop to think about it, I don't understand it either. Hell, I don't think anyone who would stop to think about it would deny the shame in it.

To make it all even more shameful, humans have been so bad in keeping up with their house cleaning that our neighbors are even starting to complain about the mess. Many believe that the Earth has indeed sent out a distress call that all alien beings are responding to, to help us remedy the situation we find ourselves in. This assumption is partially true, but not as some may think. But at least some correct communication is being put out on the reasonings of alien efforts here.

But take note, they (I should say the good-guys) are not here anymore to help clean up Earth, to them it is too late for that now. At one point they did try to steer us in that direction, but it has gone beyond the Earth's capacity now. The bad-guys have been influencing some people to clean up the Earth as much as possible. I am told that they are willing this onto people to help themselves, because if the planet goes to waste they will have nothing left to govern. If all life dies here, and the Earth becomes uninhabitable, what would be the point? If it is unsuitable for the life already here, that may also be true for any foreign life to make this a home either.

Then what would be the main focus of the good-guy's presence here if it's not to help the Earth out? What would inspire me to feel that I need to speak out so much to the public in such a dire felt manner? It is because now, with all that has been said and done by the beings that I work with, there is only one thing worth their continuing presence here, saving our very souls.

I have heard from several people that some churches are preaching that UFO's are flown by demonic beings. That they are working with the anti-christ to confuse the followers of Christian beliefs. That by their presence they are creating even a new following, so that they will be worshiped by those who do not have a faith.

Sadly, there really is a problem in our skies.

There are a lot of crafts being flown out there by beings that are under the wrong influences. Would I call them demons though? Not outright, but I'm sure they are the very ones that acquired the name in the first place. I just wish that I had a better word for them though, but calling them Shadows does imply their true nature and their characteristics.

There are so many ways to have this message be spoken of, but it's so very difficult to translate and modernize similar old teachings to make sense today. I sometimes think about how I might first present the material I've received, along with my recollections of my existences before this one. How I might make clear examples of where things stand today and how one might see these things, and of course the many arguments I will have come my way in the face of these seemingly odd yet revealing truths. I wonder how I'll respond when met with the guaranteed static from people when I talk about these things, and it hurts for me to think of at times. But my memories of my dedication to my purposes and reasonings upon first agreeing to come here, wins highly over those thoughts.

More than anything I really want to be able to relate the importance of the information about the beings that are now abundantly present in our society. I especially want to bring focus to the Gray beings that are portrayed most of the time in everything from the movies to bumper stickers. What has happened to them can easily happen and is happening to the human race. The more people get into their material worlds and pretend all alien talk is fictional, the more the wool gets woven over their eyes. People are getting tangled and they remain blinded and in limbo without even realizing it.

...he Shadows are the puppeteers to the Grays, and I do mean all the Grays that are performing odd experiments and examinations on people. No room for wiggling out for those that may consider their Gray friend as being one of the few good ones that I mentioned before. If they are taking any part in an experimentation being done to you now or in the past, that's no friend I'd consider.

Most stories we hear are about the Gray beings, and now I've learned that they have ties with the Shadows. Then if these beings are under Shadow control, how are they able to access people of this Earth? Human people are made in God's image, as its been learned for aeons, but so have other beings. So then how could it be that such a thing of darkness can touch the likes of beings from God?

The answer is simple, we are falling to the Shadows as well as the Grays did. No one is perfect, we all have our weak moments, but these beings are able to get at so many, a lot of the time. That just is not a mishap or coincidence, it is a part of who you are if the contact continues to happen in this manner. I know a few people that would probably question me about why I would say that they welcome such a thing of horror into their lives. Especially since it is usually something that gets passed down to their children.

Don't worry, it's not as cut and dry as it may seem, but then it is in a way still too. I'll explain with more clarity. There is a matter of choices being made to allow these kinds of contact to happen. How that could be, only you know your true essence and if you can be persuaded to some extent to think or do something a little off-center. Sure we all do some things that are not always approved of, but we do know ourselves and whether or not we catch things quickly or are easily fooled.

I myself have even been held in the presence of Grays and others, so I am not totally void of their contact either. The only difference is, those beings are not able to actually control or physically experiment on me. Most times I awake immediately when they approach, I then will them away, keeping in mind that I won't let them touch me. Often I get help

from outside myself to get rid of them too, because
prayer rolling over and over in my mind to keep the
light will appear and literally push them out. I wish I was strong
to always have them far from me, but the one thing they have going for
them is shear persistence. They just never give up, they seem to always be
looking for a crack of weakness to crawl in.

So to be totally void of having dealt with these beings at some point is
hard to come by. But if they are actually getting from you what they want,
and it's reoccurring, that's when they have a hold on you and you need to
change that.

As for children getting this "gift" of experimental abductions, I have
already explained part of the reasons behind these occurrences. There is a
thing called innocence that is being intruded upon at times by the
Shadows. But I also have to state, children are evolving and making decisions for themselves much earlier than in previous generations, which may
add to their commitment of themselves to the Shadows early on.

As adults and parents, we like to try and compare today's kids to ourselves when we were children, but we really can't. They just aren't the
same, physically or emotionally. Why would evolution cease now when
there's evidence of it occurring in the past with different ethnicity's and
how their bodies adjusted to the regions in which they lived? A recent
study has even found that our youngsters are going through puberty as
young as 8 years of age. We think kids are acting like they are grown, when
actually their bodies are telling them they indeed are.

Kids today know more, see more and act on more things than most
have done in the past. One can tell this is true by just looking into your
kid's eyes or turning on the television to see what today's kids are up to.
There seems to be two sides of the spectrum to what's going on with children lately, with their faster maturity rates and growth spurts.

Some kids are using their keener senses to become more primal and
instinctive in creating victims to their impulses in doing vindictive things.
Everyday it seems we are seeing more and more crimes and cruelty

occurring amongst our most precious resource, than ever before. Often we look in the cute little round faces of our children today and watch them open their mouths and spew forward such garbage to where we can hardly believe our ears.

Then there are the kids who are using these newly evolved talents to become some of the most intelligent, creative and caring humans we have ever seen. There are many kids out there, who are pretty hip to what is going on around us and are taking action to correct some of these things. Things that us so called responsible adults have neglected for far too long.

As one can see, speaking out on the alien and UFO topic cannot be solely spoken of without involving so many different factors. There are too many ways in which alien intervention has had the opportunity to be involved. It's not such a foreign idea if people had known how to address these modern day happenings of alien abductions and compared them to the tales of centuries past of demonic harassment, possession and influences. Traces of these influences can be seen everywhere, if you think on why so much has been allowed to go so wrong for so long.

The Earth is just filled with toxins that we put there, but the toxins are there because we didn't have a heart in the first place. Where were our hearts? Was this the beginning of the negative influences in our lives? If so, then this must mean that it has continued in some form from the beginning of our very existence, with the tempting of the serpent in the Garden of Eden.

Getting back to children again, with their bodies evolving prematurely perhaps it's setting off a chain of confusion in their new lives. I would then think some choices in influences may have been made quickly and poorly and the Shadows easily gained some new ground. Then of course, as I have recalled my past life connection to one side, perhaps these children also are not what they appear to be and have had pre-life ties to their alien interactor from the other side of the tracks.

Whatever it is it's easy to see currently, that we are losing the war, and Cafth and others like him know it. But you don't have to be an alien to see that revelation. We are right in the heart of it all, just shaking our heads wondering what the world is coming to.

I always hear the thoughts that a few people can change the world, and that's a great thought to have. There are some movers and shakers out there making a difference, and we primarily do have a great new generation of kids coming up. Many people don't care to recognize their young voices, but there are hidden angels and helpers amongst them that will shine brightly when needed. Most importantly if people want to see the age of a new dawn and overcome what we are facing today, all people need to make the effort and not stand idly by.

I have worked in servicing customers for years and I have dealt with good and bad customers. No matter how nice and sweet the few customers I would have in a day, it never made up for the several rude ones I had. But I tried to convince myself of it anyways, that my days were really great because of those few that pulled me through. I really needed to focus on the good things so I wouldn't have to think too long on the bad. Thinking good thoughts did help me to see a brighter day. But ultimately, I was not seeing nor dealing with the problem at hand:

Those few bad people really bothered me, and it bugged me that they had that kind of disposition and I wished I'd said something to straighten them out.

That's a similar attitude that I see all too often, people let things that bother them continue. I mean of course one can't go at every person that rubs them the wrong way, but a change needs to be made if something is truly an important issue and it eats at your soul. We all think, "Let those good-natured people deal with the hungry people of the world. Yeah, they'll take care of it, that will ease my conscience."

I've been there too. You almost have to do that to be able to fall to sleep at night.

Now when I speak on a scale of billions at risk of losing their very souls, I think a bit more concern should be leant to this problem. I hate to sound like a preacher, and it is always my goal not to. But the fact remains that a place that resembles the likes of Hell is not only a possibility, it is a threat, and I can't help but to look to awaken others to this reality. I do this not to strike fear into anyone's heart, but to help inspire the courage for people to take this problem head on. If you let the darkness touch you, it will engulf you when the time of change arrives, and it's approaching quickly.

8

Mission Impossible?: *Getting Down To It*

When I first got the notion from Cafth that I was to write about my experiences, I admit, I procrastinated a little. I really was a busy student and did not know where to begin. Plus, I really just needed the time to think long and hard on the implications of this whole thing. So maybe two and a half weeks after the intent to write a book was in place, I had an odd yet powerful awakening.

I was working at my part-time job at a local grocery store in the bakery department doing my usual tasks. It's a peaceful job, worked around my schedule, paid the bills and gave me the health insurance I needed with just 12 hours a week. Absolutely perfect for my class schedule and various other ambitions I liked to work on.

On this particular day nothing was on my mind, as usual I'd gotten to work a little late and threw on my apron to help out some customers. I remember grabbing at a bag of rolls to throw a twist-tie on it, when I had a strange and strong feeling come over me. I had the unmistaken feeling that someone was watching me. Not just one set of eyes either, but many, more like billions!

I remember looking around with a squinty-eyed look on my face trying to figure out what the heck was going on. Then almost immediately, I heard the screams and felt the immense sorrow behind those watchful eyes. It was as if the very foundation I was standing on was a big pane glass window.

"They can see me!" I exclaimed to myself in the front of my mind.

I felt totally uncomfortable. I felt pain and concern being related to me throughout the rest of my shift. It was so overwhelming, and yet I was understanding of what was going on at the same time. I could not wait to get home so I could share this highly emotional experience with Amanda.

"It was like the souls of the people that have been drug down with these Shadow beings, are wondering what's taking me so long to get started! I never felt so pressured and saddened before in my life! I know it was them, it had to be, and they really needed us!" I rattled on to Amanda, filling her ears with the tremendous revelation I had that day.

Amanda and I both saw the need to talk to Cafth about this immediately. Amanda can contact Cafth on her own, but she can do so more quickly and easily if I help by leading her into relaxation. So I began to instruct her on relaxing her body by imagining being engulfed in a white light starting from her head to her toes, setting the stage for us to begin another chapter into the real world.

Cafth pops in, "Yes, you called?" He then spread a smirk across Amanda's face.

"Yes we did. Practicing your jokes on us again I see."

"Yes. Human humor you have taught me well."

"Cafth. I really need to talk to you about something that happened to me today. While at work I felt as if there were billions of eyes watching me and…"

"You know that they can see you…" He replied candidly.

"Oh my God. It was those people…their souls or whatever, watching me and wondering about my intentions on doing this book!"

"Yes. They are able to see what is going on and it saddens them. They try to warn others not to follow their same path, but most do not listen."

"How are they able to influence people?" I asked.

"You felt their presence today did you not?"

"Okay. I see your point. But why exactly do they have such an interest in this book I'm supposed to be doing? I mean, I see what you are saying that they are trying to warn others not to follow in their footsteps. But hey, there is no guarantee that I will ever get a book done and if I do, who knows if it will ever get published!"

"So many meanings in your questions, one at a time (sighs)…always getting ahead of yourselves."

Cafth then took a deep breath and began saying, "This book will be as a warning for those that comply with those negative beings. People will be made aware of what is going on and what may happen to them. It pains those that are suffering at the hands of these beings, to see that their loved ones or even mere strangers are at risk of joining them in their misery."

"This book is a book of importance for all who are concerned for their souls and well-being." Cafth concluded.

"In actuality though, how could such a book help those people that are already there. Those people got there because they lacked a little heart and soul in the first place. So why such a loving concern now for people here who don't really directly concern them?" I thought this was a smart and logical question to ask.

"They now realize how they were misguided and yet are still trapped. Writing this book is one of the first steps to ensuring their freedom."

I thought, "Me and my writings can have an impact that large on an age-old situation?" Self-doubt always creeps into the picture. But now I needed to redirect those feelings into actions and more helpful questions instead, so I pressed on with Cafth.

"How can all this being written down, help them get out of their situation Cafth?"

"Humans are not alone in their struggles with these Shadow beings, we are at war with them to stop their mission. It is making people aware of what is going on, that will let them know not to run from their help."

I interrupted him to clarify his meaning, "What, that we should know who our enemy is and who our knight in shining armor is?"

I suppose if we do not know the face of either, how would we know what direction to go towards when it comes down to it? Almost sounds like a choice between good and evil. But we make choices everyday that can have a negative or positive result on things.

Cafth went on to explain that once they are successful in forcing out these bad guys, Cafth and his companions that work for The Source will release those souls that are trapped. That even they will have their day to learn and perhaps live again in another form, that is, if they look to The Source for guidance upon their release. Not exactly Biblical from what I recall, but I do remember something about the end times and even the dead rising for some sort of judgement. I don't pose to know about the whole Bible or the whole scene of things to come, but this all sure seems to ring with similarities in what was written and what I've now learned.

Cafth said that there is a dark crystal that needs to be destroyed in order for this release to happen, but it has already been captured. I do not fully understand what is meant by all that and he pretty much said that we are not expected to, so I left it alone.

Cafth went on to reassure me, "We already know the impact that your book will have so do not concern yourself over minor things. I wish I could tell you, but I would get into trouble. If you only knew where all of this will lead you." He then made Amanda squirm with delight.

Okay, so I was not to worry everything would fall into place. That sounded simple enough, but oh, I was still dying to know. It was nice to hear that they had so much confidence in me. But I still had a hard time in understanding why they were so sure of all of this.

Yes I knew who I was now, but I was still in this human form with lots of human doubt and emotions. I have always had this dire fear of becoming successful since I was a child. I somehow felt that if this were to happen that too many people would follow my lead or something crazy like that. I know what it sounds like, having such high expectations of this sort. But this was something different, a feeling that I was almost born with to be careful not to allow people to look up to me. At times, having this instinct was really distractive for me because it made me painfully shy as a child and still continues to persist in certain situations.

So at a young age I decided that I would avoid having any kind of stand out role. While in elementary school through high school, I suppose you could say that I did not hang out with the "in" crowd. I felt most comfortable with those that did not go out of their way to be noticed, but used their minds instead.

I was in the accelerated classes, where students were more in tune with their capabilities and those were my friends. The only *outstandish* thing I engaged in was Forensics and a couple of plays, but it didn't take me long to lose the nerve for that too. I had mainly done those performances to express my humorous side and that was about it.

Cafth knows all this about me and I wanted to purposely address my avoidant feature, so I asked, "Why would people believe me anyways? I don't have any direct proof and I don't want people to look up to me as the "all knowing wizard!"

"You have done this before." Cafth said patiently.

I was stunned from his response. "I have? Where?"

"In Yugoslavia. You influenced many people there. You were very successful in your mission."

"Yugoslavia?" I thought aloud. "Who was I, and what did I do there?"

"That is not important. All you need to know is that people will recognize you for who you are. People will see that it is us that speak through you. That it is our message that you are relaying and not a mere single individual's opinion."

Just then Amanda herself broke into the conversation, which she does time to time. She does this whenever she wishes or is shown something interesting and wants to interpret it.

"Oh my God Heidi! There's so many!" Amanda exclaimed.

"So many what?" I was confused and startled by her sudden outburst.

"He's showing me you, standing and giving a presentation to a lot of people and behind you are rows and rows of spiritual beings! Oh my God, I can't believe how many there are!" She ended.

I didn't know what to say to that. I knew that Cafth had popped back in after her last statement and he came forward and defined what he had shown Amanda.

"She has an army behind her." He asserted.

"An army?" I said, and then was silent. "They speak through me now at times don't they?"

Something clicked inside of me that seemed so familiar and awakening at the same time when Cafth mentioned that. I suddenly remembered several instances when I was talking on the subject of UFO's or aliens to someone, I would sometimes feel light headed and find it difficult to speak. Like so much would be filling my head on the topic that it was like a thick soup in my brain. Words, instances, facts and emotions all in one, felt like they were being brewed in my skull.

I used to think that I must have hit something sensitive on the subject that awoke spiritual or alien ears that would try to inhibit me to prevent the discussion. Then while I was inhibited, my thoughts would just build up into that soup, or something. Then I thought it must be something similar to how it is when people gather to talk about ghost stories. You get super sensitive and jumpy where all your senses are heightened to what's going on around you, so I thought maybe it was related too. I didn't know, I was just trying to explain it all away somehow.

But now I knew what it was, these army of beings were just trying to help out. I explained to Cafth that I now had realized that they had stepped into several of my conversations and what would happen when they did. They would just flood my mind with so much info that it became difficult to direct my words smoothly at a good pace and focus.

Cafth immediately responded that he would tell them to be more subtle in their approach next time so I can speak easier. But he also mentioned that it was up to me to speak with them and work with them. That they were always there for me to look to for comfort, guidance and a variety of other things that I may need in my journey.

Well that was definitely comforting to know that I was not alone on this, outside or internally. Nor were any of the people who reside on Earth, alone in this secret battle that they were not fully aware of. I understand that people have held tight to the belief that the devil was just waiting for them to fall, and I have learned to respect that belief more so than ever thanks to some of the teachings I have received lately.

No, I don't believe in the exact ways that these kinds of notions have been taught in church, just because I have seen otherwise. But, one thing that I have been taught in my theology courses in the past, is to always respect people's beliefs. I had a hard time swallowing that one because I know what I know, and I cannot retract and pretend that I don't have a clue about direct spiritual matters from my ties and memories. But what made this all easier was to know that even though some religions had very different practices, they still had the same goal.

It seemed to be that the general religious goal was to shed light on the dark things around them and find their true essential selves, so that they may someday return back to their source. That is my same goal so I am not all so different after all. I don't claim my belief system to be a religion or anything, but it is the path that I have chosen and I follow it religiously, if that counts.

If all our spiritual seekings are aiming for the same goal, then why are we not working together on this more? It seems that people feel that there is a distinct line between the writings of the Bible with its beings of light and darkness and the modern day beings or aliens of today. It seems almost as if you *have to* choose sides and be a believer in the church or a believer in the round (or triangular) ships. Believe it or not, both of these ideas and phenomena exist and co-exist, and neither are going away.

We have to learn to respect each other's ideas and backgrounds so that we may gain strength in our numbers. One thing these negative beings would hate to see in us is unity, they don't even practice it amongst themselves. Ever hear of a band of criminals work in harmony? Then imagine how these beings work together.

These beings are placing their bets on us to not figure them out, but I have the download on them that I am willing to share. They are not to be taken lightly nor doubted for their power, they are a power with many faces. Some faces that you may have heard about and others that you may not, nevertheless it is a forever changing face that everyone should be made aware of.

9

THE FACES: *THE REPTILIAN BEINGS*

Who or what is exactly is at the helm of all this negative jargon I'm speaking of is important to know. However there are actually quite a few involved, so it is nearly impossible to even cover how far this all goes. Also, I don't want to inspire a witch hunt for those that you may suspect of being in conjunction with these negative beings I'm going to mention here. None of your direct actions would make much of a difference anyway since it is an inner battle that person must come to terms with on their own.

This whole thing has all been going on way before any of us were born, so this is an ancient, rotten dilemma that we cannot deal with on our own. I've said it before and I will say it again, my goal is to just make people aware, not to pass judgement. There are so many varying degrees of people's involvement and the direction they are heading in, that there is no way any judgement would be just or fair.

I mentioned earlier how these Shadow beings can take on many faces and come in different shapes and forms and have other beings work for them. One such being that works with the Shadows in addition to the Grays, are the reptilian looking ones. Cafth has informed me and Amanda that their first given name by some ancient culture here on Earth, was "Dadish" (DAH-deesch).

These beings stand anywhere between 6' to 8' feet tall. They are varying degrees of green, have a scaly appearance, with yellow, snake-like eyes. Many have reported having sexual relations with these beings and shockingly enough, some say that they even enjoy these conjugal visits.

Then there are those that say they fear these nightly visits so much so, that the person tries to rid themselves of their fear. People involved with these beings have found that once these Reptilians see you have lost your fear they make their exit. So it would seem that these beings feed on the energies of our fears.

Not only can that be concluded, but they also play upon sensitive issues and our weaknesses. Sex is one of them, our sense of control is another. What these beings are doing is that which is the equivalent of a rapist. It's popularly known that a rapist's actions are all about control and power over another individual.

I found it odd at first that these Reptilians would have to find pleasure and power in such a human way. But later Cafth would explain to me, "They are interested in taking away what humans value. They take it any way they can, power is their goal."

"Just power? They do this and all this dirty work for and with the Shadows, just because?" I asserted.

"What drives humans?" Cafth slipped out cunningly.

Well he had me there. That statement alone prompted me to explore the subject much further. Cafth was right.

We are a power driven society that is always looking to get ahead. We may claim to be on the same side of something or have similar enough ideas to label us to be one way or another. But in retrospect, we are essentially out for ourselves. Unity? Perhaps in name and gesture, but we are individuals that cannot all be defined under one definition.

Cafth said that there is no unity amongst the Shadows and their coworkers, which I suppose explains why there seems to be no single "devil head" or leader as we may define one as. But if there is something close to it, you can bet their hold on their workers is on shaky grounds.

These Reptilians or Dadish, are simply out for their own personal gratification as well. If I didn't know any better I would say humans must be related somehow or they really are human people's mentors. I have learned that nothing is of coincidence, and people sure do have a lot in common with them.

I have heard some refer to these Reptilians as having nothing kind in store for mankind. I've heard one researcher present the idea at a conference, that the Reptilians were at one time angelic guardians for the people of Earth. But then they grew weak and lusted for humans and somehow became damned by God. It was also pointed out that the idea of a serpent or snake, is always referred to in the Bible as being something of evil.

Once again though, we must be careful not to stereotype a whole race. As with the Grays, the non-abducting and non-intruding Reptilians are not with the Shadows and their dark mission. I in fact had an encounter with a Dadish that was quite pleasant. My biggest fear, before I met this one, was that I would see an alien eye to eye and I would freak out or something. I had many encounters with partially visible beings and the ones I encountered in dream-state. But to have a real good look at one face-to-face while conscious, was something I wasn't so sure of.

This incident happened to me as a result of an attempt to get over my fear of speaking at the science fiction convention I had mentioned earlier. My friend Bob, who first recalled the Shadow People's purpose with me, also happened to be a licensed hypnotist. So I asked Bob for his help in possibly putting the suggestion in my head that I would not be nervous about this presentation. He suggested a less persuasive route in where he would find the underlying cause of my fear so I would face it and possibly get rid of it. So I agreed and we headed on our merry way to relaxation and searching for the cause.

I fully remember saying to Bob that it wasn't working, that I didn't feel "down" while under this supposed hypnotic state. But I told him to continue talking to me anyways to see if it would help still. So Bob had a little talk with me about what my fear was and etcetera and after about 40 minutes of talking, we ended the session.

After sitting up, Bob asked me how I felt about my fear of doing the talk. I remembered everything that was said, I answered coherently when he asked me a question and so I began to tell him about doing the talk and how I still felt nervous about it.

Then suddenly I remembered something and exclaimed, "I saw aliens!"

Needless to say, Bob hadn't a clue what I was talking about. I went on to explain, "I saw something hiding behind a dark doorway. I almost overlooked it in my mind's eye, but then I went back and I told it that I saw it. Once it realized that I had seen him he stepped forward and out of the shadows to show me who he was. He was a large, bright green reptilian creature, that was maybe 8' feet tall. He had yellow eyes like a snake, and he had a deep pinkish-purple stretch of skin that went behind his neck around his shoulders. His entire body was full of large folds of loose skin that hung so much, you could hardly tell one leg apart from the other."

"He stood there with his neck and chin up so high in the air, I could sense his pride and conviction in himself. I know how strange this must sound, but all I could think of was how absolutely beautiful he was." I confided to Bob.

I remembered that I did not receive any telepathic message directly from this being, but I was given the sense of why he was there. His presence was that similar to a loving father that is very strong, but lacked the "know how" to show his love. That his presence alone should suffice in letting me know that I was not alone, but that he cared enough to be there.

After his image went away a whole slide-show of different types of aliens were shown to me in motion in my head (except for a dead alien that was shown to me laying propped against a wall in some cluttered warehouse). It was not like a memory or anything either, this was something that was going on right then and there. I was being given a tour of some of the different species that are out there and I wasn't afraid of them. There I laid, and I met with several beings that were asked to show themselves to me and somehow I was at peace the whole time.

Well, I got over my fear of seeing an alien eye-to-eye and I think that was the purpose of the whole thing for me. The odd thing was, the Reptilian face of that being stayed with me for 2 weeks afterwards. When

I say that, I mean his face was forever just to the left of my normal view with my eyes wide open! The most fascinating thing about that phenomena, was that his image was comforting and welcomed. It's a shame all of this didn't get rid of the fear I was aiming for though.

Cafth later told me that this being was learning to know humans. That he was one of the few that Cafth and his people rescued from his planet before it was taken over by the Shadows. He did not conform to the Shadow's ways, so there may be few, but not all Reptilians are negative.

A characteristic that should be dutifully noted though, is that Reptilians also have the gift of deception, physically. They are capable of taking on other animal and human forms. The thought that they are able to do something like that should really start the hair on the back of one's neck to rise.

What on Earth are they capable of doing if they look like everyone else? I could hardly imagine, but I see the possibilities are endless. Who knows, perhaps that lone person that strikes up a riot on the streets did not have anyone's best interest in mind at all. How could we ever be clear to determine whether or not the face of a person is not a person at all?

The answer is that, there is no answer.

All I can say from my experiences with these types of "people" is that they are not to be fooled with. I have been in contact with three individuals that I and a couple of friends have concluded to be one of those hidden beings. Two of these people have been identified as being a form of Reptilian and the third was never quite figured out.

To say that these few reptilian people knew who they really were, there was no doubt in my mind. But I also know that like in my situation in recalling who I was took some time, some of these hidden beings are not fully aware yet of who they are either. They play a role of being like a double-spy, they are not fully intact with their memories so they can't be spotted as easily for what they really are. So they may feel inclined to get closer to some people as myself that are on opposite ends of this battle, and unknowingly they are storing what they learn and reporting it when they do their routine visits to home base.

The first hidden being I took note of, I encountered through my two friends again Jim and Bonnie. They had introduced me to a woman that I will call Lynn. She was someone they had recently gotten to know through a small group in their town where they discussed metaphysical topics and the like.

I went to one of their group gatherings at Jim's house where I met Lynn after everybody kind of dispersed into different discussions with each other. Lynn came straight to me right away and started asking me about myself. To this day, it tops my list as one of the weirdest conversations I have ever had.

Lynn knew where I lived and asked me an oddly worded, yet leading question, "So where have you lived in Milwaukee that you liked the most?"

I started saying, "Well I really liked the one place I lived on the eastside…"

She then cut in and said, "You know I used to live in Milwaukee, right on Knapp street."

I said, "Really? So did I, that's the place I liked the most!"

Lynn then went on without making any reference or motion to what I had just said, "So what high school did you go to?… Ya know I always used to drive by this new high school that they were building called Vincent."

I then stopped and looked at her and said, "That's exactly where I went."

Lynn still showed no response to my reaction when she named the very high school I had gone to.

This conversation seemed to go on forever and it continued on in the same fashion. Just before I was about to say or answer something she would answer it for me, and as you can see she wasn't being vague either. When a person knows specific names and pronunciations, feel reassured that they are not just shooting around in the dark!

After each revelation she told me, I would remark by saying something like, "Yeah, me too!" Then she'd follow up my statement with a big blank expression. It was as if she were looking right through me stealing what was on my mind and just eating it up. She showed no pleasure or personality for that matter in what she was doing either, she just did what apparently came naturally to her.

At the beginning of the conversation she had asked for my phone number to discuss some metaphysical topics, which I saw no problem in doing. But by the end of the conversation I wish I had not given it to her after she said she would be calling me. She said it with almost a smirk on her face as I stood there totally dumbstruck as to what just happened there.

After everyone left, Bonnie and her daughter came up and showed concern for me asking if Lynn had done anything weird. I told them how the conversation went and how strange I felt. They apologized for not warning me about her and her odd abilities. They also went on to describe some even stranger instances they had with her that made my experience seem small in comparison.

Jim and Bonnie both had conversations that sounded a lot like the one I had with her. They had also had odd instances in where they called Lynn's home and job where someone would answer in a very deep scruffy voice, which is a common characteristic of Reptilians. Whatever the voice said Jim nor Bonnie could decipher what it was.

Then one time, instead of hanging up Bonnie said, "Lynn, is that you?"

The voice then became recognizable and Lynn's voice changed and acknowledged Bonnie. Just a little too odd for my taste, and not too normal of a response again.

Out of curiosity, Bonnie had Lynn's license plate run by a friend to see if that would shed any light on exactly who Lynn was. Bonnie had her fair share of meeting odd beings and having stranger things happen, so she knew how to go about figuring some things out. Well her findings didn't help to solve who Lynn was, but helped to decipher who she wasn't. The plate came back being registered to several different last names of Lynn, one could only speculate why. I suppose someone like her must be versatile.

Another interesting character that was of the Reptilian sort, is someone I will call Mark. Mark thought he was so totally together in fooling those around him as if he were like everyone else, but he was mistaken. I had only met him briefly once before and the next time was to be on a road trip, which took place a few years ago. Myself and several others that were going, were highly uncomfortable with the idea that Mark was coming along too.

It was hard to identify, but we knew that something just wasn't right with that man and he would later prove us to be correct. He was a very tall man with an upright posture and he had this twitching thing going on with his neck. After spending more time with him on the trip we noticed that his neck twitching would happen only when he got near us. I don't think it was a nervous thing, condition or bad habit either, it was much stranger than that and it changed up quite often.

Once we'd arrived at our distination, those that we came with were anxious to see what it was that Amanda and I had come in contact with. At the time Amanda had just started up with communicating with Cafth and we had mentioned the thrilling news to all of them. So we all got together one night and I got Amanda in a relaxive state and she began to talk to Cafth. I should mention that this was the first time she had ever communicated with Cafth in front of others too which is something she still doesn't feel comfortable doing too often.

Cafth began moving Amanda's head around as if she were looking at the different people in the room, but she always has her eyes closed and covered. Since she began, Mark was making an odd motioning with his hands as if he had an invisible ball in his palms. One of the people there then asked him if he would stop because it might interfere with Amanda, and he obliged. After the contact with Cafth it was explained by another that Mark was able to draw up energy between his hands, for what purpose I am not sure of.

The first thing Cafth did after looking around was tilt Amanda's head forward in the direction Mark was standing.

Cafth then muttered, "I know you."

Mark remarked slyly, "I know you too."

Cafth quaintly uttered, "Who do you think you are fooling? We can see through you, and they will see you for what you are soon too."

That was all that Cafth had to say about Mark. I didn't see Cafth as outright attacking Mark or anything. Cafth didn't raise his voice or stress anything about Mark, I just didn't know what to think about what he meant by his statements. Especially since at that time, Amanda and I didn't know so much on the subject of the Shadows and their companions.

After that session with Cafth, he said that he would try to have a craft swing by for us all to view. So immediately afterwards, we all went outside to check the cloudy night skies in hopes of catching a glimpse of a craft. So there we all stood, when Mark comes up slowly behind Amanda as she stood alone at one end of the parking lot we were in.

He then leans his 6 foot plus frame down and whispers gently in her ear in a nasty tone of voice, "I think your friend is devil-isssh…"

Well we didn't get a clear view of a craft that night but Mark later would prove that he was indeed the *devilish* one. He showed a friend, while we were there at the hotel, how he could make whirlpools in the swimming pool with the energy he could conjure up between his hands. That talent was not what made him devilish, but his purpose in doing this trick was. He was trying to impress upon my friend to lure her into his greatness, I suppose you could say.

Mark also was a being who liked to elicit sexual vibes, which was also something Lynn was reported doing towards males or females. There were instances when Mark would walk into a room and several women present would admit that somehow a sexual thought would pop up in their minds about him. To these women, these thoughts were totally foreign to them as if they were not even their own thoughts. He'd also been known to approach women and men alike in a sexual manner, even children for that matter.

While on this same trip, one of my friends had a waking dream of seeing Mark in his true form as a Reptilian. He was in front of the hotel room meeting with another Reptilian with whom he seemed to be discussing his situation with. The situation being, all of us on the trip with him and where he stood with us and what he was doing.

After Mark finally became successful in hitting it off with one of my friends on the trip, he revealed something about himself that was totally remarkable and I would suspect not a common practice amongst many of his kind. He admitted that he was involved in a secret war going on. That he was in charge of teaching aliens how to act and pretend to be human! Well with that neck thing going on, I think he needs some refresher courses himself. Then going after men, women and children to hit on, I'd say he was not too bright either.

No boundaries, what a scary thought.

These beings do not see a wall, they just see the wall as extra footing leverage to give them a boast to leap over and into our lives. The characteristics I have just spoken of are major indications as to who some of these horrorific beings are that are among us. But I am sad to state there is another touchy characteristic that is undoubtedly pronounced in their behavior, high interests in the UFO phenomenon.

Once again let me make myself clear that this does not mean everyone that is interested in this subject is some kind of odd creature. But UFO's and the talk about them is something that is a real issue with these Reptilian beings. So much so, that several of them are in the forefront in **supposedly** uncovering facts about the UFO phenomena and related topics. What a coincidence that Lynn and Mark both had an interest and were involved in attending and arranging group meetings of this sort. Are these beings really out to help? Some swear that there is a conspiracy of misinformation out there about UFO's and the related topics. Maybe it isn't all the government's direct doings after all.

I am not pointing the finger at any person in particular. But could I, in actuality say and name a few? Yes I could. I wish there was no such thing as defamation of character because let me tell you, I would be the first to open my jaws and flap my gums. But keep in mind that my main goal is to tell the tale so it will at least be put out in public view. But I will try to be as thorough as I can in telling my next story of a certain individual that is very well known, without revealing who he is. Only he will know who I am speaking of in reading this. For it is only he and a select few who knows what he tried to do and failed.

What name shall I call this "man" for the story's sake, Damian, that's a suitable name I think, it reminds me of a certain movie-but anyways. I cannot go into detail as to how I came about meeting this Damian since it may reveal who he is. But I will just mention a story in brief that I think will suffice in giving you a clear understanding as to what I was up against with this sorry excuse of an existence.

Damian is the kind of guy you could take home to your dad so he could ask you, "What are you crazy? He's nearly twice your age!"

But nonetheless, Damian was very professional, presented to be educated and descent to hang around with. Plus he had a similar passion I did in being fascinated with the UFO phenomena, he just happened to be practically making a living out of it. Once again he was tall and had an upright posture, one that I would depict as looking very anal and uptight. I say these things about posture because this being, including Mark, always looked very uncomfortable in their body's to say the least. Perhaps it is a tight fit for them, since these Reptilians are generally 6 feet and over.

In the beginning, I just could not understand why Damian considered me as being such a big asset to have around when he was near or in town giving a talk or whatever. I mean, here I was a typical college student with nothing much to offer and here he was a well known UFO researcher. Something was up with him, he wanted something, but I just could not put my finger on it. Being curious, I hung around to find out what he was after.

But I didn't hang around silently. I was continually mentioning to my friends in the MASE group that I felt that somehow he was trying to benefit from me being around and associated with him. I had no proof, but I would get my answers later. Damian wasn't being a pervert or anything with me either, he treated me fairly. But then after knowing him for more than a year, he did ask me out to dinner in a round-about way.

He asked if I would ever go out with a guy like him. I literally laughed out loud in his face the first few times because I really did not take him seriously. Then a couple years passed and the question arose again and persisted for a few months. By this time I did realize he was serious and I could not laugh it off so easily.

After a problematic relationship had concluded for me, I finally did agree to meet Damian for dinner, with honestly no intentions of even starting anything with this much older man. More like meeting a friend for dinner even though I knew he was interested in me, but I still saw no harm in meeting him. To be honest if I avoided all the men that even had a remote interest in me, I'd have few male friends. It just seems to be a common occurrence for some reason, not to sound like I'm some sort of "hot stuff."

The day before we were to meet, Amanda and I had a discussion with Cafth. A discussion that took a dramatic turn which ultimately saved my life. I barely had begun to get in depth in conversation with Cafth when Amanda suddenly fell silent.

She still seemed to be receiving some kind of information, so I waited patiently. But then she started breathing heavily and seemed to be almost in a panic. There was only one other incidence when Amanda had trouble breaking contact and that was with an odd looking being she had never seen before. In that incident she appeared agitated also and I helped her back away from that being by guiding her to push her way out.

So when Amanda began showing agitation this time I immediately thought that something else had barged in on her, which happens but very rarely. So I offered to help guide her out, this time Amanda did not say a word, but instead waved her hand telling me to leave her be. She continued to huff and puff and choke even. She appeared to be trying to communicate, but every time she tried her words choked her. It was a strange choking sound too because there was no voice in the choking at all as if she had no voice box to choke as someone normally does.

This went on it seemed, forever. Every once and awhile I would ask her if she was sure she didn't need my help and she would still wave me off. Finally it ended.

She sat up immediately saying, "Oh my God Heidi, I gotta tell you…(choke)…!"

Her words were still gone. She continued, "Oh, I was told I wouldn't be able to speak to you about this, here give me some paper then."

Amanda then began to scribe down what was the most incredible account I had ever heard.

She wrote, "I was shown the restaurant where you and Damian are going. You got up to go to the restroom, he ordered wine and put something in your drink. This was to make you fall to sleep so he could take you to his world, underground. Heidi, it's horrible it smells like sulfur, it's ugly, and there are several Reptilians there and one was Damian. He feels he is so successful in getting you since you are a part of those he considers to be an enemy. He has killed you by taking you there and you are trapped!"

Amanda stopped writing and I read it, and as I did she kept repeating, "Don't go Heidi, don't go."

What do you say when someone tells you something like that? So many things were rumbling through my mind, but I wanted to confer with Cafth to see what that was all about. So Amanda went back into meditation later and we asked him about her vision.

Cafth said, "That wasn't me who showed you that. I do not show futures. It could have only come from one thing, The Source."

"Whoa, you mean The Source was in direct connection with Amanda and it was to warn me about Damian and show what Hell is like?"

I really didn't feel worthy to have *GOD* come outright to warn me! So I went on to ask, "Is this mission that important that The Source would take the time out to help and warn me?"

"You are there to represent all of us and our mission. We often warn those like you, sometimes they listen sometimes they don't. It is up to you if you want to listen or not," Cafth said.

Well, I was one to listen and I called Damian almost immediately the next day.

I told Damian, "I really don't want to ruin our friendship, so let's just keep things the way they are."

I'm sure most of us have either heard or had to say that one before, and Damian was really cool about it. There was silence at first then he said, "Oh that's fine I completely understand."

Suddenly there was a beep on his phone, he clicked over then came back to me and said he had to go, that his publicist was on the line. But he said he would call me right back.

If I had any doubt about what Amanda had related to me, they were gone after what happened next. As soon as I hung up the phone with Damian, a force hit me so hard in the stomach and chest, that I flew back half-way across the room! It felt like Jean Claude-Van Damme had gotten a running start and did one of his famous two-footer kicks on me! I went back and all the wind had been knocked out of me and I embraced my stomach and chest while heaped over.

Amanda was standing in view of me and ran over asking me vehemently what happened. I really could not speak right away because I had no air to speak with.

But with the first wind I think I muttered something like, "That son of a @%&*#!!! He hit me!!!"

I really don't know why I said that because I did not see him or anything else hit me. But I knew he had something to do with it, the timing was just too perfect. To top it off, he never did call back and that was not like him. I guess I spoiled his plans and he put a dent in mine as well since I was sore for a couple of days. The first day I could barely even stand upright it hurt so bad.

After an incident like that you would think that I would run and hide, but I didn't. I in fact went to a gathering I knew he would attend and smiled right in his face as if nothing major had happened. I wanted to tell him so bad that I knew who and what he was and that I would continue on in what I needed to do. But Cafth had told me that it would not be a good idea to reveal this, that it would jeopardize me even more.

Cafth said, "Damian knows that you know, and that is all that needs to be done."

I still did not fully understand why I was a target for so long with him, there are others like me all over. At the time, I hadn't a full picture as to what all my purposes were or anything like that.

With the right questions and persistence I finally got a clearer message from Cafth who said, "Damian saw that you did not see who you were yet or your potential. He could see the army that surrounds you. He knew if he could control you or your destiny, he would control your army and purpose as well."

It's always about control and power, isn't it? How sad.

Still to keep on the brighter side, it's good to note that there are plenty of other beings around that are not malevolent. But for the most part, those beloved Reptilians are not to be trusted or messed with. I later found out that this Damian is a sort of commander of some of these Reptilians. That he is very powerful in the underground and above ground as well, especially in the UFO community.

I was lucky to have had a higher power to save my hide, but others may not be so lucky. If one suspects someone not being quite as they appear to be, don't confront them but keep that knowledge and steer others clear of the individual on the sly. There will be a lot of people that fit into the physical characteristics I've described here, but they may have odd body language due to various impairments also. But do know, for those who wished they'd get the opportunity to meet an alien, odds are you already have. So do tread carefully, when you are uncertain. Above all else, without sounding too "cheesy", higher power discretion is advised.

10

THE MIB = *THE MOST INCREDIBLE BULLSH*TTERS*

Thanks to the movie "Men in Black", or MIB's, have been a big topic in recent times. Hollywood has had a ball in making a comedy out of something so serious once again. But don't get me wrong, I enjoyed the movie too. It's just that I think another needs to be made to show what the MIB's role in our society really is.

Many victims and witnesses of the UFO and alien phenomena, have been threatened and intimidated by these mystery men and their signature suits. These MIB's will come to witnesses homes and tell them it would not be beneficial to their health to reveal what they have experienced or witnessed. Then they will sometimes outright say what harm they will do to the person or shove them around to make sure their message is clear.

So there is no doubt that this MIB thing is associated with the UFO phenomena since it is they that mention why they have come. They sure do go through a lot of trouble to convince regular citizens not to get too ambitious in spreading the word on this stuff. I'm sure a lot of those people feel as I do, in that they are not personally worth the bother for such a big fuss.

The one thing the movie did get right, are the threads these dark invaders are said to wear. These men always dress in black suits with black ties, and sometimes with hats and sunglasses. The color of their skin is said to be somewhat of a pale, tan color. If their eyes are seen they are said to be somewhat slanted and at times are seen completely black, showing no whites of their eyes. Their voices are often described as being very deep,

95

rough and sinister sounding. Their trademark vehicles are large black cars that appear to be brand new. That is, new looking, but about 20 years outdated. These cars always have tinted windows and are often classified as being a Lincoln car model.

One question everyone asks, those who know about the true phenomena, is if these MIB's are human or not? I really wanted to get some answers to this one myself, so naturally I resorted to Cafth for a little insight.

What I got from Cafth was a big, "No."

I needed a little more elaboration than that and so he went on, "These are non-human beings."

I responded, "What do you mean "non-human," what kind of beings are they then?"

I at first thought that they were human at one point and were somehow made to do the work of the Shadows. But after thinking about it, it made sense that they had never been human. These MIB's were often described as being very stiff and irregular in their movements. The idea that they did not move normally made me think of that uncomfy thing with the other non-human beings, the Reptilians posing to be human.

Cafth interrupted my thoughts and said, "They are of the Shadows, and are enslaved by the Shadows."

"Do you mean these MIB's are the form the Shadows take when they want to come around to bother us?"

"They can come in any form. These are Shadows themselves and they take the orders that are given to them."

"They are enslaved by their own?"

"Yes. That should not be surprising. I have told you before that they spare no one, not even their own."

With a policy like that, it is no wonder that we have not fared well against these beings individually. They did not even value their own kind, so why would they care about us! The next thing I wanted to touch on with Cafth was what these guys were up to. What was it that they were trying to accomplish by seeking out witnesses and harassing them?

Cafth went on to answer me, "They are here to stop the truth about us and others. If no one knows about us or the Grays, then the Shadow's mission with the Grays can be a success. No one will look for help with us, or fight them. Silence, that is what they are aiming for and if they have it, they can move around more freely on Earth."

I added, "Silence, but they threaten and do whatever else to get that silence. But still, I have not heard of too many stories where they have actually done something to the people they threaten. Why do they bother to threaten people if they don't follow through?"

"They do. But why should they do it themselves when they can have someone do it for them?"

"You mean they get someone else to do their dirty work?"

"Yes. They influence someone else to do whatever it takes, whether it's to give that person static about everyday things or even if it means to kill that person. Then that person, that allowed themselves to be influenced and continues to throughout their life, is indebted to the Shadows. The Shadows then get their soul when they pass."

Unbelievable! These MIB's want to take down as many people as they can at a time. I suppose if that is your goal, it would make sense to not actually follow through on the threats yourself. Why do that if you can get someone else to do it and get an extra side-order of "soul" to take home?

The next thing that popped into my mind was about the government's knowledge about this. I wondered if they knew that citizens were being threatened and executed at times at the hands of these being's influences. I somehow thought for sure that this particular phenomena might not be fully understood by our government, or maybe I was at least hoping that. Because if they knew about this, it would be a total outrage and absolutely treacherous of them.

"Does the government of the United States know about what is going on with this MIB thing?" I asked.

"Often times it is someone in service to the government that is influenced to follow through on the threats of the Shadows (MIB's). Part of the government knows about it and other parts do not."

So it was treachery indeed, but still I felt I needed to clarify what he was saying. "Okay, but I remember you saying how these Shadows deceive, where a person unknowingly falls victim to their schemes. So does the government know about how deep they go in taking our afterlife?"

"Some parts know and others do not." Cafth reconfirmed.

Cafth then went on to discuss further the extent of the knowledge that some government people are aware of, that I will discuss in more detail later. The important thing to relate now about these MIB's is that they are a force of influence at all levels, even in government.

I wanted to know more about how these beings have been getting by in doing this influencing trickery. Personally, I would think they would be hitting a brick wall with me. So I find it hard to imagine that they are so successful in "leaning in close into someone's eyes and putting a hypnotic suggestion in them." I am sure that is not what they do exactly, but it still had that hypnotic feel to it.

Cafth projected, "The Shadows have been here for a long time, influencing is what they do. That is their power, but if you listen to your true inner voice you will not even hear them."

This was an interesting revelation for me to hear about. I really thought that these MIB's were much more of the brawn behind their threatening words. But I had heard that they would pretty much scare a person half to death and then make their exit. Now I knew that words were their main weapon, which could be out loud to one person and deep inside another where they could cause them to do harm.

I know that I would be shaken if one of those tan, scruffy voiced MIB's came to my door. But for some reason these guys are seen as being comical or something since that movie was made. People seem to like to think that this was all just the creation of a writer with a great imagination. I wish that was true. But heck, now these MIB's are so popular they're responded to with great affection. Now there's even a cartoon for our kids to idolize them and know them as the defenders of Earth. Heros of all things, darkness termed as "beings of the light."

Television and the media has a way of making us all numb to what is really going on in the world. But I will tell you one thing, if one of these guys comes to your door and it isn't Will Smith, don't open it. There have been way too many people claiming to have had a run in with these guys for this whole MIB thing to be discredited. All the evidence that's out there to prove this to be a true phenomena, and it only takes one comedy to hush it all up and lessen it's chances to ever be mainstream knowledge or news. The visitations by these beings have not stopped though, and the stories are out there for whomever cares to listen.

One of the most incredible stories I've personally heard about the MIB's was one I heard from a friend at work I'll refer only to as Mike. Mike knew that I was into this UFO business so it was not an odd thing to mention something to me on this matter, although he had never done so previously. But he related an incredible story to me this one afternoon, that I will never forget.

Mike told me that he was watching Unsolved Mysteries one summer evening in 1997, and they were doing a report on the mystery surrounding the MIB phenomenon. Mike found the show interesting and informative and continued to watch the report. The next day it was really rainy out, but Mike still wanted to go apartment hunting and check out a place in his neighborhood.

In driving around looking for a particular address, Mike came across two large black, older model, Lincoln cars that had just pulled up in front of a house.

Mike starts, "It was the weirdest thing. As soon as the cars pulled up it was like everyone counted to three and they opened their doors all at the same time! There were four guys in each car and all eight of them opened their door at exactly the same moment! They all had on the black hats and suits and they all wore sunglasses and here it was hazy and raining outside."

Mike continued, "They all walked up to this house and about half went to the back of the house. The way they walked was in perfect synch with each other's too. I was just slowly driving by looking for an address and I wanted to get another look at these guys. So I went a little past that house they were at to turn around and come back. Just as I was passing the house again they were starting to pull away. I was kind of blown away by all of this since I had just watched that show about them and there they were!"

I think Mike's account is really unique in that he was not the target of this MIB visit. He just happened to be driving by and spot exactly what he saw on television the night before. Perhaps the media can be helpful in bringing some things to light, so that people know when to take notice of something that's a little out of place. Often times I wonder if the sharp increase in television shows documenting UFO phenomena are specially targeted to slowly make people aware of what's to come.

It is odd but understandable that some of this stuff is just too weird to be believable until you witness it for yourself though too. I don't know if people do this just to protect themselves or to hide from the truth of other realities. But what if people do open up to some of this stuff, as a whole? Perhaps if we all do there will be less stories to be labeled as an unsolved mystery, but see the mystery for what it really is, a fact of our universe.

11

ANGELS EVERYWHERE: *PEOPLE ARE NOT ALONE*

There has been evidence of unearthly beings visiting us for centuries. But it seems that some of the lore has been around for so long, people have just become accustomed to the old stories they have been told without really thinking about them much. But lets take a look at one of the most commonly known unhuman beings, angels.

I hope I am not the only one who has thought of how ridiculous it is that people believe in a human looking entity fluttering around with wings. I say it's ridiculous because these angelic-spiritual beings are so much more acceptable for people to believe in than a being like Cafth. I don't see much more of a stretch for a person to believe in one over another really. But I do know that there are indeed beings with wings out there, and I also know that there are beings with varying body types, sizes and colors, that are just as kind.

Some say angels were once humans that did good deeds and earned their wings. Others say these angels were always messengers of God and nothing less. The funny thing is, why do we accept these truths as if they were our own?

Out of curiosity, I often ask people how it is that they came to their conclusion about the existence of angels and how God runs things. More often than not, the response I get is, "Well the Bible told me so." That's fine. But is the Bible believed only because it is tradition and passed on as such, or because their faith relies on the words of men inspired by God from a couple of thousands of years ago? I do hope people are following with their hearts and not from memorized verses and traditional rituals to do, only to *show* they are faithful.

I understand how some feel that millions of people cannot be wrong, that there are just too many people who instill their faith in the Bible so it must be believable. But in the times before Jesus, the main religious beliefs were not that of the same Christian beliefs we know of today. In fact Jesus had a heck of a time convincing people that his views were clearer than the current beliefs and that's one of the great reasons why they killed Him. Now I am not trying to suggest that I don't believe in what's said in the Bible, because I am learning more and more everyday that there's more truth in it than anything.

I am just saying don't shoot down the messenger or a new message before you thought about it a little first. The men that wrote the Bible were inspired by a higher power to write the words they felt were true and we take their word for it still, thousands of years later. I am also inspired by a higher power, and I mean God or The Source not Cafth, to convey the messages that I believe to be the truth.

What I don't get, is that people believe that God did indeed inspire the words of the Bible back then, but now He just doesn't have the time to give the same or similar inspirations? In my college theology classes, I often liked to spark conversation towards this subject too. People in my class would talk about something they saw on television where someone claimed to have had a vision of Mary, Jesus or angels. They were so content that those people's experiences were authentic, to some of my class-mates, that proved the existence of angels and whatever else their religion permitted them to believe.

I think they believed it because it was safe and within a normal accept-ance range that is built in our society and religions. They believe in the words of someone so far away from themselves, but when I spoke up in class and said I saw God or The Source, heads turned away. I wasn't saying it to sound "all-knowing" I was just sharing as everyone else was encouraged to do, in a humble and orderly manner. I even went on to describe The Source and everything about how it appeared to be a swirling mass of light.

A much later lesson in that class taught us that the number one symbol of "God" across the globe, in assorted primitive cultures, before the teachings of the Bible, and before communication linked different parts of the world, was a swirling mass of light. Just as I described it to look like in my memories. So I know I am not the only one who has seen The Source in this day and time or any other time. I never got a glance from anyone during that particular class period and I don't know if it meant that they didn't make the connection or choose to disregard it. I suppose it's easier to believe the pope or some little girls in a remote area that they might have seen God, Jesus or Mary, but not the person sitting next to you. No, it's not surreal or unreachable enough to be believed.

Now how ridiculous does this all sound? I am boasting if I claim to have had a "God experience," but it is gospel if someone on the opposite side of the planet claims the same? I suppose it was because I have this UFO thing going on that made me less believable, and some of my classmates were aware of this. But then again, I don't think so.

I did not describe God or The Source as a big man, sitting on a throne, floating in some clouds. I told my classmates just what it was, a large beautiful light with billions of individual souls that equaled one will. I did not have any preconceived notions that has stuck with me of what God should have looked like, so nothing clouded my judgement. I did not need to see a coverup that was easier for me to accept, so I got to see God for who and what it is.

This thing about angels being the only messengers of God, and God sitting in the clouds on a throne is neat too. But as Amanda once said to me, "First people thought God was in the sky, sitting on some clouds. But once we could reach the clouds we saw that nothing was there, but clouds. Then we reached the moon and nothing was there either."

So where does God reside then? I always get the smart alec response from different people saying, "Why, He's everywhere!" But that was not the case in the Bible, when people praised God, their hands and faces were turned up towards the sky and they even built a tower to reach Him. He was known as the God from above, and that has always been known and now it's going to be taken back? Now He's just everywhere?

I of course concur that His presence is felt in every crevasse but, if God's throne is not in the clouds then what are we saying, He resides on another planet or floats around in outer space? Well, where I saw The Source it was surrounded by beautiful stars against the darkness of space. For me, that is where God is, and yes He is everywhere too. If people want to still envision God as sitting on a mighty throne, then so be it. But even various churches acknowledge that some of the concepts of their traditions and faith are a bit outdated, like that divorce thing.

So then perhaps some of the other ideal thoughts that surrounded around God are outdated too. The idea of a throne, why that was an ultimate privilege to be sitting on one, way back when.

"For God to rule, He must have had one to sit on," is probably what was thought then. If He is everywhere, why sit?

Then back to the idea of angels with wings. There are some beings that have wings that I have heard about in the UFO community. But not all of these beings are too angelic like, some have even been described as being a kind of Reptilian.

The beings that I have heard of and seen as being closest to the description of angels, are the aliens that some call the Nordics. These beings are generally 6 feet or taller, male and female. They are said to be strikingly beautiful with blonde hair and odd-blue eyes. Sometimes when these beings move they kind of glide along, slightly above the floor. Now if I had seen something moving around like that back in Biblical times, I would suspect it had wings on it's back whether I'd seen them or not.

I did ask Cafth if he could tell me if that was how the idea of winged men, called angels, came about. He said something like, "Yes they were seen then and they are the ones we call Guardians. Sometimes they do appear with wings, but often not."

"Guardians," that was a name that Cafth has used on several occasions to describe who or what was in our apartment, protecting us from the Shadows that hung around. Amanda has not been as fortunate to catch seeing these beings as much as I have. I have usually seen them as streaking masses of light, and they vary in color. They are usually pastel colors in yellow, pink and blue. When the Shadows came around Amanda could spot them right away, but I was usually so amazed with the pretty Guardian lights I could barely see the Shadows when they were near. Amanda on the other hand was so terrified by the Shadows, that was all she could seem to focus on.

The Guardians pure form, I was told, were these multiple colored lights I'd see. But we did not know for sure, what solid form they usually took on until we decided to bring it up with Cafth. So to make sure my assumptions were correct, I asked Cafth what these Guardians looked like and he said, "They often take the form where they appear almost to be human and have blonde hair and blue eyes."

So perhaps the title "Guardian Angel" came into play that way and why angels have often been portrayed by artists as blonde and blue eyed. I later asked Cafth if these Guardians were just as people have always depicted them as being protectors, since they were for me.

Cafth responded, "Yes. They are amongst all people on Earth. They influence good things and protect against the Shadows."

I was told that myself and Amanda are heavily protected by the Guardians against the Shadows. That at any given time there are at least five of them around us. On a bad day, when we have been bombarded by Shadows in our shared space, we have had as many as forty Guardians around. Days like those could be really stressful at times. We were not always aware of what was going on until we both would have trouble falling asleep and wake up to find massive shadowy figures in our rooms and streaks of light. It looked as if there was a mini battle at times, going on before my eyes. Even after that all goes away, neither of us can fall to sleep most of the night. Cafth said the Guardians would keep us filled with energy so we couldn't sleep.

He said we are weaker when we sleep and the Shadows can influence or have greater access to us at those times. That filling us up with energy was no joke either. I noticed that whenever those eventful nights happened and I tried to fall to sleep, my heart would suddenly start racing, giving me an adrenaline rush that would perk me right up again.

These Guardians are said to be around us all, but to see their light or them as a solid being, is a rarity. I have only seen one of them as a solid being before and it was at my job. A young woman, blonde and blue-eyed, was standing at the end of the aisle in the grocery store I was working in. I was busily waiting on customers, but for some reason I felt her presence and looked down the aisle straight into her eyes.

I was surprised to see this woman just standing there gazing right towards me. I was still busy working and waiting on people, so my attention had to turn towards them and I just brushed off whatever it was I felt about that woman. Before I knew it that same woman was standing right before me, just behind a few customers I was waiting on.

Once again she had a locked stare on me and I tried to glance back every chance I could. I was walking up and down the length of the counter I stood behind helping out some customers, when I saw that the woman had stepped right up to the counter. In between my pacing I stopped to ask the woman if there was something I could help her with. In getting within a few feet of her, I was just in awe.

Her face was completely flawless and she had such a beauty it seemed that there was a distant light glowing about her face. I don't fully remember what she was wearing, but for some reason I had the impression that she had on an odd jogging suit. But the one thing that truly stood out, were her eyes. They were of a distinct blue that had a light of their own that I have ever yet to see since. Her eyes were also a bit larger than I have normally seen on any person.

When I asked if I could help her she shook her head lightly, still staring at me, and then backed away slowly to the other end of the aisle. She then stood there a few moments more still staring at me, then I turned away to finish my customers order and she was gone. It was an odd but wonderful experience that I would be lucky to have repeat itself. She elicited such peace, love and patience all at the same time, it was just incredible. This happened to me about a year or so before meeting Cafth and I asked him if she was one of the Guardians and he did confirm that she was.

It's funny that you will never see or hear much about these beings. It seems that the media only likes to focus on what is strange, odd or traumatic. Even UFO researchers don't seem to regard visits from kinder beings to be legitimate contact, or contact worth looking into. It's all about the hype, which is why you mostly see pictures of the more sinister beings such as the Grays and Reptilians, everywhere. Even Hollywood likes to disregard anything that might be too normal and accepting.

The movie *Fire in the Sky* is a perfect example of how some important facts are left out. I went to a UFO conference held in Springfield, Missouri where Travis Walton spoke on his experiences that the movie about his abduction and disappearance was based on. His story is based on how he went missing for several days after he and his co-workers came across a UFO out in the woods where they worked as lumberjacks. His friends were suspected of his murder, until he unexpectedly reappeared several days later, dehydrated, starved and confused as to what happened to him after walking up to the craft.

It was disappointing to hear that the meat of the movie, when it came to the aliens, was made up. Travis said the makers of the film, "Hollywood-ed it." Just wonderful.

He said that of the Grays he saw, they were the typical looking ones we have all heard of, not the big lugs that drug him through the ship in the movie. He also stated that he has never recalled having any experiments done on him. Most of all, the movie never mentioned the aliens he had the most contact with, the human looking, blonde hair, blue eyed ones.

Now why cut that part out? Is that too unbelievable that a very human looking being was involved in this odd abduction? Is that the reason that when people ask me if I have seen the "creatures" that fly the UFO's, they have a smirk on their face?

I suppose it is easier to laugh at and poke fun of something so odd and un-similar to themselves. Say for humor's sake, that there is life out there on other planets. How silly would it be for one of them to think that Earth had way too much oxygen to support any intelligent beings? Sometimes I still ponder that possibility when I hear the uneducated remarks I encounter at times.

I don't want to say with certainty that the beings that Travis saw were or were not the Guardians, but I am not aware of them taking people in that manner. It doesn't seem to fit their purpose, nor correspond to what they usually do. They are also a more spiritual being like Soforus, that does not require the use of a ship to get around in.

Then why were these beings in the form that the Guardians usually take, I wondered. Well I knew that the Shadows took on different forms, especially this one in particular. Imagine being taken aboard a UFO and find yourself surrounded by small Grays, totally not what you are used to and you freak out a bit. Then you see this practically human looking being walking towards you, and you find yourself calming down. That form could surely reassure you and make you feel better about your situation and for you to be even more accepting and easier to work with.

Cafth has said that the Shadows liked to take that form to place blame of some abductions on other races that look similar too. That it helped add to the confusion as to what may have happened to you, thinking that some super blonde humans got ahold of you instead of aliens. You might just relate it all to a dream, and not try to seek out answers and find out what's hiding in the shadows of your bedroom. That action would be to your disadvantage, but help out a great deal in the grand scheme of the Shadows.

I will just make it noted here that any beings, including the Nordic types that are working with abducting aliens are not the good guys. To watch the Grays take a person against their will, fill them with terror beyond belief and sit idly by? I'd lean more towards them not having the best of values.

In relating back to the Travis Walton case, I cannot ask specifically about other's experiences. Not unless there is a lesson to be learned, or I have that person's permission, or if they are present when I'm speaking to Cafth. So I could not get direct information about his incident and I think that's best, because it lets people define experiences on their own that they read about or have seen first hand.

The next story I'm about to mention is very interesting, especially because of the fact that the Guardians have not been advertised too much. This account was told to me by Amanda's uncle, who resides in Puerto Rico. I went there to experience island living for a three week vacation in the summer of 1997 along with Amanda.

One evening we went to visit Amanda's aunt's home and I got a chance to start talking on my favorite subject. I had heard there were a lot of UFO sightings in the area so I first asked her cousins what they had heard. At the time, the Chupacabra stories were just starting to die down a little.

Chupacabra means "goat sucker" in Spanish. These were small (appx. 3 feet tall), hairy, red-eyed creatures that roamed Puerto Rico, killing several animals by sucking their bodily fluids out through small puncture holes. Many people on the island were terrified of these sightings and it was a critical topic on their news for awhile. I did ask Cafth about these creatures and he was brief to say that they were a mistake that was being handled.

Amanda's aunt related a story about a Chupacabra sighting near her work that had happened sometime earlier. Then one of her cousins spoke of a UFO sighting she had with her boyfriend up in the mountains. Their stories were interesting enough, but nothing topped what Amanda's uncle Joseph had to say about a visit he had one night.

Joseph had a separate home built behind his wife's home where he would go when they had a quarrel, a hide-away I'm sure most would appreciate at times. The night he had a visitor, he was staying in his home alone, which was something he said he did quite often. One night as he was sleeping, he said a tall alien with blonde hair and blue eyes sat on his bed and began to talk to him.

He said, "The alien told me that I was sick and needed to go to a doctor. Then he said that my son had a serious problem with his blood and that I should take him to a doctor right away too! So the next day I went to the doctor, and that was when I found out I had a bad blood infection and that my son had leukemia!"

I was shocked that her uncle knew to call this being an alien. Here he had lived high up in the mountains of Puerto Rico all his life where religion and cock fights is more commonly spoken of. But he still thought of this being as an alien and not an angel as the Bible so often depicted these kinds of helpful beings! So I asked Amanda to translate for me and ask him why he called this an alien.

Amanda then looked his way and related what I asked. He answered her back and I was astonished to hear his answer. Amanda was too, since she could hardly stop laughing.

His response was, "Well, when he came in the room and sat down on my bed he said, "Hello, I'm an alien and I am here to help you."

Well there's no mystery there where he got calling him an alien from! I had to laugh at the response and Joseph did a little too, but he still was quite serious. I would be too, since this encounter saved his child's life and possibly his own.

Angelic like beings, just like the ones in the Bible. But you don't have to look the role to play the role. From what Cafth had told me about him and his companion's roles, I once asked if he was like an angel then or something too.

He smiled at that remark, but said, "That is a human term, I am alien. But we have been called many things."

So when you think of angels next time as being only some type of man-bird, try to see that it is no more different than realizing that some other "odd" looking beings could play the same role. Maybe it was not God who made us in His image. Maybe we were so stuck on ourselves that we decided to depict Him in our own image.

12

AIDE's = *ANGELS IN DISGUISE AND EVOLVING*

Cafth has made it clear to me that they personally are not able to, nor allowed to directly interfere with what happens on Earth. This is why they send down beings like themselves to be born into human form. That in order to change something with Earth, they must be experiencers of the Earth and life process.

Cafth explained that a bit. "It is against the rules to come and impose something to change from an outsider's perspective. Which is why I am not to influence you directly in the choices that you make. You are not under my control, you have the right to choose to do what you want with the information I tell you."

Through Cafth and our own memories, Amanda and I knew we were sent down here to complete some tasks that were connected to The Source. For Amanda to hear and recall that she was what some may compare to as being an angel, was no surprise to her. For years, Amanda depicted herself as a "fallen angel" in several of her art works. Not "fallen" like the devil, but more like where she had to leave the heavens to accomplish something. She told me that she had always felt as if she had come here for a reason to assist in helping people. But she could never figure out how she came to be here and the exact mission she was to accomplish.

In seeing some of her artwork, it seems as if she felt the same way I did when I remembered where I came from. She always depicted herself as being a little sad that she had to leave where she came from, but joyfully took on the duties given her. In one large painting, she shows herself as a winged angel looking back sadly from the blue tunnel she passed through to get here. Another huge sketch shows her as an angel, retrieving a star God sent her and other angels to search for.

One incredible revelation about Amanda's possible angel connection came Amanda's way more recently in July of 2000, when she went in for some chest x-rays due to some odd health problems she was experiencing. She did an array of other tests also and they all came back normal.

"Except one interesting thing," her doctor said curiously. "You have some extra ribs, and they aren't in the usual area either." He then showed the x-rays to Amanda who described to me the extra ribs being between the 4th and 5th ribs approximately and angling up to her collar bone as if for extra support.

The doctor continued, "Yea, they are curved differently and are formed odd. Almost, **bird-like**. I've never seen this before, or ever heard of it, it's very rare if at all."

Now what that all means, I'll leave to the imagination. But when I heard it, I referred to all her drawings of herself seen as a winged angel. When she was first told this by the doctor it didn't even dawn on her about her angel perception of herself until I mentioned it, I don't see how she could have overlooked it. But to me it was staring us right in the face, perhaps her memory served her better than she even knew or wanted to know.

I know when I recalled agreeing to leave The Source, I was overly anxious to do so. Upon exiting, I immediately wished to go back though. I was saddened, I was no longer in this warm pool of love and voices of deep thought. Cafth said that upon my coming to him and my volunteering to come down to Earth, that he had warned me.

He went on, "I told you that you would not have all the energy you possessed now. But you are the adventurous type, so you did not listen anyways."

He said he told me that I would be stripped of my energies, where my light would be dimmed, and I would be more on my own here. But I could see myself being like that, all ready to just go for it since it had such great purpose. But I usually do listen to good advice, as myself now anyway.

Cafth went on to tell me how as a child, I would try to escape my body to try and come back to them. As a child I had epilepsy with unexplained origins. He said when I had a seizure those were my escape attempts and they had to constantly be bringing me back. I can't say my own memories serves me to recall all that he mentioned, but either I outgrew my epilepsy or grew up enough to know it was not for the greater good to keep on trying to leave.

All I know is now I'm proud to say, that I gratefully accept the challenges that are here for me. But I admit that there have been several instances where I have just wanted to give up in trying to open up anyone's eyes. I used to be so anxious to talk on the UFO subject to let people know that aliens were really around. I now don't even see that as being effective nor important for me to be the one to prompt a conversation on the topic. I feel that I am just supplying the means for people to know the truth just in case if they care to find out, they can.

Freewill and free range of thought. That is what most successful societies are built on and that is how it should be. There should be no one who feels they can dictate down to another or give them ultimatums if they do not follow through on something.

If people ask to hear what they should or should not do, that's called advice and I may be caught in giving that as anyone would. But one has to beware of some advice givers out there, because not everyone is in your corner to see you through anything. Advice may be given or hints of why some things may be the way they are, just to see to it that you are thrown off the trail of the true agenda at hand.

Cafth once stated, "The Shadows are playing by the rules (of no outside influencing without permission), but they are cheating (go figure). They are making a hybrid that is half alien and half human so they are a part of the Earth and it's occupants, and the darkness. They will be made to follow the orders of the Shadows. They will not be able to make their own choices. It will be an enslaved existence."

had always stressed to me that no one could be influenced or harmed by the Shadows unless they were weak at some point and somehow allowed it to happen. That some people had even given their permission to be involved with them before they were born, just as I had, but for the other source. Then here it is revealed that permission will no longer have to be sought since a being can be made and taught to be a servant to their cause from the beginning.

I almost feel sorry for these hybrid beings. I have heard stories of abductees that have had alien children and how they get to see them periodically when they are abducted. These children often have stringy hair, pale skin, and large heads with big, but often human eyes.

It seems that the Grays, who appear to be the ones mostly creating the hybrids, do not know exactly how to handle these children. So often times the abductees are sought to teach the Grays how to care for them and hold them. Sometimes the person abducted is made to judge whether or not these babies have enough human characteristics. As I was told by one such person, "If they passed or not."

What would happen if they did not "pass?" What happens to these children then? Another friend of mine, Susan, happened to stumble across that answer unknowingly. Susan, has a daughter by the name of Hope, which is neither of their real names. Susan had been suspecting that her daughter was having some kind of abduction experiences because odd marks would appear on Hope's body and then vanish. This mysterious occurrence was even witnessed by their family physician who had no explanation for this happening.

Susan got in touch with a mutual friend of mine named Karla who was a licensed hypnotist and involved in the UFO phenomena. Susan wanted to find some answers about Hope's odd markings, and after seeing a television special speaking of something similar, she was certain it was somehow alien related. So Susan agreed to have her daughter regressed by Karla to find some answers. At the time Hope was approximately 5 years old and she proved to be a challenge to regress, so not much got accomplished through that route.

Susan then volunteered to be regressed to see if she recalled anything ever happening to her daughter during the night hours. Susan was a bit skeptical that she would be able to recall anything because she thought she was too sound of a sleeper. She thought this of herself because she had never been able to recall having a single dream in her life!

Skeptical or not, Susan was put down with ease by Karla. Susan then began to relate the unbelievable fate of some of these hybrid children that did not pass by some sad standard. Susan stated how every night she found herself leaving her body. She would then go to guard odd looking children to make sure they didn't leave the city they were confined in (which explained her dreamless sleep, she wasn't present). Susan said that she volunteered to be born here on Earth so that she may give birth to a child that would rescue these children, Hope.

Susan said, "These children are very thin and small. They are not really children, they are older, but they are still small like children. They won't grow anymore than they already are, they don't look right so they are kept here. They are too weak to escape on their own, but Hope will guide them. (She begins to sob) I don't want Hope to leave me, but I know she has to. This is what she was born to do, they trust her."

Sounds as if this was some kind of dumping ground for those hybrids that did not pass a certain breeding standard. It is good to know though, that even those beings will be spared at some point and rescued from the holding they are kept in. Hope was to be their Guardian and guiding light, which leads me to believe that they are not necessarily born loyal to the Shadows. I would see that as being a possibility since they were half human, so they must be groomed and raised to think that they have no other choice but to be Shadow's workers.

When I first heard of the information Susan recovered in this session, I really could not understand the meaning of her recollections. I was still in a state where I did not know what this alien thing was all about. What really amazed me was Susan's reaction to what had happened in her session. She didn't even want to know what she said.

Before awaking she asked Karla to make her forget all that she had said, because she couldn't bear the pain of knowing her child would have to leave her to help those children out. Her session, which was done about four years ago, was videotaped and she was given a copy of it. From the last that I have heard, she has yet to be able to watch it in it's entirety.

If there is to be any sort of goodness in the purpose of the Grays creating another race, I would like to see how. I am sure I am ruffling a few feathers out there of those that are involved in the abduction experience and aid in creating these children. Some of these people are my friends now and who knows, may not take to kindly to me afterwards. I can't help what it is I now understand about the hybrid creations going on now. I can only hope that some of this makes sense, and might go further than just being blown off as judgmental babble.

Time and time again I have heard women claim to recall being raped or impregnated by alien visitors, only to have the life in them taken away. The movie called *Intruders* based on a book by Budd Hopkins by the same name, depicted a story of a woman that experienced that happening to her.

She was noted as being pregnant, the placenta was intact still, but the baby was gone. The woman was horrified to have her doctor explain to her that her body supposedly reabsorbed her baby, what a horrible explanation to give. Why don't our scientist just say it like it is, that they haven't got a freaking clue instead of blaming it on mother nature as they often do when they can't explain something. Bones can't even be digested fully by my dog in his stomach where acids for digestion are for it to take place, but a uterus can?

Personally, and common sense in thinking, I see nothing beautiful in losing a child to some unseen creatures. If it's for the greater good as some of these hybrid creators would have some believe, then allow that individual conscious choice to help out or not. I wonder how many takers they would have to assist in given up their kids and using their bodies as a baby machine for an army.

After attending several groups and conferences, there has always been the question, "What are these aliens up to, already?" In the pits of our stomachs, I'm sure most of us felt it could not all be good. But then there was that certain benefit that would come in different forms that would make some think it couldn't be all bad either.

Some people claim to feel refreshed and enlightened after an encounter, then of course some are just left in a state of shock from the terror they just endured. Then there are others who claim to have been blessed with gifts like psychic abilities and healing powers. I also have some psychic abilities where I can sense some things and predict others. But it is never something I have been able to control, it's spontaneous like a deja vu. Perhaps with practice I could be more productive with it, but I don't think that's its reason for being there fully.

I have also been able to heal in matters of energy level between me and Amanda. We discovered this after a discussion with Cafth and Amanda felt drained, as she often did. She then reached out and grabbed my arm in a jokingly manner and said, "Give me some of your energy, I'm drained!"

Afterwards I felt drained, so I turned and grabbed her and took it back! We were laughing hysterically at what was going on, that it was actually working. Since then, sometimes we exchange energy between us after speaking with Cafth, but we have never tried this on anyone else or in any other instances.

I went to Cafth to ask why it was that some abductees were receiving some psychic and healing gifts, if practically most of these Grays were supposedly evil.

He said, "They have their own agenda in mind for doing that."

Then I began to think about when I asked Cafth if there was something he could give us to be able to prove to people that the experiences we were having with him were real. Cafth said that is not how they work. That to intervening where they would shock people into conforming to follow them.

Cafth shared, "Those that are to see the truth will realize it and see that we are the force behind the words and that we work only for The Source."

For some reason his humble response made me think of the thoughts I had as a kid about how God used his powers. In Sunday school I remember being told that God used his resources to make miracles, that he did not just make something happen in a flash. My teacher then gave the example of how God parted the Red Sea for Moses by using the winds. That he was a humble God in his approach to make things happen.

But here, the Grays are giving the appearance that their abductees are given gifts of healing because they are in touch with them? From what I have learned of these people, when they go to lay their hands on someone to heal them, the Grays come right through the walls to assist in the healing. I thought maybe some of these Grays were the good ones, but Cafth said they do it to make themselves look good so that people would follow them. He said it is actually the beings that are doing the work and not the person. Of course everyone cannot be lumped into one category. Some people are given the same gifts by another means or type of being.

So I asked about those other people and where and how they came across their psychic and healing powers. To me it didn't completely make sense that there were still some people, as myself, that have predominately had positive experiences and possess these kinds of gifts.

Cafth began, "The Shadows always try to influence those that we are in contact with. That is why some will, at times, have questionable experiences where you believe them to be negative. Then other times you are at peace with the encounter you are having, those are experiences with beings like us. There is always a constant battle going on. To answer your question more directly, those that work with us also possess gifts that are sometimes taught to them or that they possessed on their own. There are gifts that you two possess (myself and Amanda) that you have yet to discover as well."

A battle, even in the experiences that we have. It made a lot of sense to me, since I had a questionable experience here and there myself where it didn't feel all that positive. But I never felt as if I had been experimented on or harmed because they never seemed to be able to touch me. But I knew that something wasn't right and I knew that those were not the same beings I was mainly in touch with.

I think the variances in experiences will explain a lot to others too. I have seen many people puzzle over the meanings of some of their encounters. It is one thing to come to the conclusion that you are at all connected with some aliens. But it is a whole other thing to realize that you are having totally opposite experiences too.

Imagine being taken into classrooms being taught miraculous truths and shown serene beauty and having wonderful conversations with some beings. Then the next night you find yourself strapped down to a table having some skin scooped out of you by some other beings or ones making themselves look like the ones from the night before. I would think it to be quite puzzling and yet you might allow what's happening because you think it's the beings from the night before.

One such person is a good friend of mine and Amanda's by the name of William. William had belonged to a couple of UFO groups I'd attended and we all grew closer as time passed sharing more about our individual experiences more and more.

One evening while dining at a neighborhood burger joint, William decided to dump a mother load of information on me and Amanda. "I've been really disturbed by some of my experiences lately with a female alien," William began.

I continued to lean into my burger, looking up periodically to hear the rest of what William had to say.

"Yeah, well I have been having sex with this alien woman. More like, I'm being raped by her."

My burger suddenly got lodged in my throat. I looked up at William in what must have been a most sorrowful look. I knew what that meant and I could tell that he didn't think it was a good thing either.

I thought to myself, "Should I tell him that what was happening was tied to his soul and some kind of agreement he made at some point with these beings? But I was asked to not speak on what Cafth has told us yet."

I battled back and forth in my head, looking up at Amanda seeing if she felt like giving in as much as I did. Then I just said it, "You know you don't have to let them touch you, don't you?"

I could tell William was puzzled, so I went on, "Somehow at some time, you agreed to let them come to you like this. You have to break that contract and know that you can."

William had told me before that he had several wonderful experiences with what he called his spiritual guides that happened to be Native Americans. But he knew they were fully connected to who he was and his alien contact. Still he couldn't figure why he would learn so many wondrous things in experiences with the guides and then be preyed upon by Grays that knew of his other contacts with the guides.

I went on to explain to William how he could rid himself of these beings and keep them at bay, which I will go into detail in Chapter #16. Later that same evening as if they had overheard our conversation, the Grays and the female Gray came back to see to it that William was still under their control. Well they were in for a shock, because he knew how to protect himself and how to get out from under their paralyzing glare now.

William was successful in drop-kicking the Grays out the door that night, but of course they would still try to take a jab at him now and then. But the important thing to note, is that William got the upper hand on these guys. These negative experiences were halted which made way for him to have more contact with the more positive beings or guides.

I also learned some good lessons with the success that William had too. That for one, what Cafth had taught me really worked. Once William had found his strength to get rid of these guys, he not only had more positive experiences he also got his memory back.

He recalled agreeing to be a part of the Grays mission, "I was sent in to be a spy on you and Amanda, Heidi. But I also recall that I was actually not a part of their kind, but a double agent sort. It was like I was sent to pretend to be working for them, only to later recall who I really was and mess up all their efforts."

Once again someone else sent to see to it that Amanda and I was not successful in completing our mission-like deal. I at first thought that I had made a mistake in revealing some of what Cafth had told us. Because right after we did, boy did we get bombarded with Shadows in full force. So that was another lesson I learned, that speaking too soon about this stuff really did put us in more danger. But I now see that it was meant for me to speak to William when I did, otherwise who knows what kind of information he may have gotten from us to report to the Grays had he not been told how to break his ties.

We all have to make a choice and make an effort to not let those other experiences happen. We have to conjure up the courage to literally tell them to "get away," and mean it too. But whatever you do, don't let any persuasion move you on their intentions. If your experience is uncomfortable and they do not stop, that is not one of the good guys, so back away.

I know that it is difficult to take all of this in, but what I am relating is not just a logical speculation. This is what the issue is at hand. The Shadows are here to influence us to follow their lead so that they can repopulate the planet with those beings that only respond to them, look to them, and welcome them as guides.

I know Cafth is no god, but he speaks of God (or The Source) regularly. In fact, I was so inspired by the way Cafth related to The Source, that I began praying again myself after years of not doing so very regularly. Cafth says he prays or speaks often to The Source to keep up on what he should be doing while on this mission with us.

He has also said that praying to The Source is one of the main ways to break your loyalties to the other source, the Shadow's. Cafth may not look like your typical "angelic being," but his heart is in the same place. He and his fellow companions, of many different species, are here to help and it seems we could use all the help we can get.

13

WWW: *WHAT WEB GETS WOVEN BY OUR GOVERNMENT*

There have been so many debates as to what the government knows about all this UFO stuff. Cafth has spoken on many topics indicating what the governments of our world do know, and what they are doing with that knowledge. But this chapter is putting that aside for now, so I can give a more personal account of what the government has done in my case and in all likelihood is doing this to others.

I personally have known for sometime that the United States government knows a heck of a lot more than they are telling. Before I even realized I had a clear role with aliens, the government knew about it. I don't know exactly whether they got their info via some aliens, or just simply saw UFO's on radar hanging over my house once too often. Either way, some government goofs knew something was up with me and this whole UFO business, because they sure did take the time to visit me every so often.

Beginning in 1989 and continuing into 1990, was the time for the census to do their rounds and tally up the population of the different people in the United States. At the time I had just moved into my first apartment with five other roommates.

One day I got a visitor at the door who claimed to be from the census bureau. She was a older lady, late 60's, who promptly put her hand out as if to congratulate me for being chosen for a rare census. She said only one person is chosen out of some thousands of people (I can't remember the number) and I was that person, Heidi D. Hollis.

I didn't see any harm in it so I invited the lady in and agreed to answer her questions to complete her little questionnaire. She said it was some kind of survey to see if I utilized any variety of government programs or not. So she began to ask me some questions out of this fairly lengthy survey pamphlet relating to that sort of stuff. The questions did ask things like if I had ever been on welfare, how much money I had in my bank account and if I used foodstamps. But then some of the questions seemed a little odd, like what were my religious beliefs, who was I dating and what were the names of the others I lived with!

Believe it or not I answered her questions, I was young what would you expect. Her questions went on for what seemed like an hour or so. Then she surprised me when she asked to speak with each of my roommates! I was just glad to be done with the questions so I went and got whoever was around.

I wasn't particularly concerned about what my roommates were asked since I really didn't know them (I answered an ad for a roommate). But my best friend at the time was staying there with me for a while, and she got questioned too. I just assumed she was asked the same stuff, so I just didn't bring it up again.

Well in time the roommate thing didn't work out to well. So I moved out with one of the girls, Jenny, that I did get along with. Jenny and I found a comfy little apartment and moved in, which was only about two months after staying at the other place.

It seemed like only a day after we had moved in and gotten our phone connected, that we got our first call. It was the census lady! "How odd," we thought that this woman was able to locate us like that so soon after moving!

I was the one that answered the phone and I asked her if she still needed something. She said that she needed to continue to do follow up interviews to keep up with any changes in mine and Jenny's life. I then said that I thought that I had given enough in the first interview and thought it would end there. But she went on saying that I signed an agreement for her to continue. I told her I did not remember signing anything. But I figured that there really was no harm in all of this anyways, so I didn't argue with the woman.

So I told her nothing had change with me and then I passed the phone to Jenny to update the woman on her status too. I just didn't think much about what this woman was about, but she did get annoying since she did call or drop by once a month! This went on for about a year before I had to move again and this time it was to my sister's house. Nothing was in my name there, so I guess I made things difficult for these "census people" to track me.

My best friend called me shortly after I moved, the same one who had been questioned before, and said that some people from the census bureau came to her house asking about me. She said that they were dead serious in finding out where I was, which kind of made her feel resistive to their questions. So she wouldn't give them any information about me.

I was really stunned that they went to such extremes to find out about me, since this friend lived in another state. At one time I did go back and forth quite a bit to visit my friend in her home state, but how did they know to go there? A call wouldn't suffice?

I couldn't understand why my friend would feel intimidated enough not to answer their questions. The sister I was living with also received an inquiring call from the census, but she did not feel inclined to answer their questions either. But I really got the chills when my parents called me with their suspicions.

I believe the conversation went something like, "Heidi, what did you illegal?"

That was one of the first statements out of my step-mom's, mouth. I was baffled as to what she was talking about since I had never done anything of the sort previously to make her think that.

"What are you talking about?" I responded.

"Some people kept calling saying they were with the census bureau and they wanted us to tell them where you were at. We asked them what they wanted with you and they just kept asking more questions so we hung up with them. Then they showed up at the door, two men and one woman, demanding that we tell them where you were. We said we didn't know. Then they got smart with us saying, "You don't know where your own daughter is?" Then they said, "We'll find her, we always do!"

I then told my parents about the strange census lady that kept bugging me with her odd questions. My parents said that these were no census people, that they were a part of something else to be that aggressive. I then remembered a phone number the census lady had given me. I had to do a bit of digging to find it, but I did and called the number.

That number was disconnected. I then decided to look up the real census bureau to see if they had a census survey like that. When I called, the man that answered said they did have a similar census where they would follow an individual for 2 years to see if they utilized any government programs. But he said there is no way that a government office can ask anything about a person's beliefs and personal business for a census. He wanted me to gather more information about who these people were posing as the census. I told him I would get back to him later on that.

I did not follow up on calling them back though because I knew that whatever it involved, it was way over their heads. In the conversation I had with my parents about those census guys, I did make a joke that maybe it all had something to do with the UFO I saw in downtown Milwaukee. I don't know what made me say that, especially because I saw this UFO two months after this census thing had already started. But it is good to note that the census inquiries did end with their visit to my parent's home.

It took three more years before I truly realized that this census thing was indeed linked to my involvement with UFO's. I hadn't been with the MASE group for long when I brought up the topic, "Had anyone ever had a run-in with government people before?"

I was just curious if there were any others that might have had a similar odd experience as myself. I would say there were about 15 people at the meeting that night and about four others spoke up. Each of them said they had some "census people" come to their home asking a bunch of non-government program questions too. All four of them were suspicious about who these people were also, because these group members knew of their personal connection with UFO's.

My mouth felt like it dropped down to my knees. I then admitted as to why I asked, because I too was suspicious about some census people that continually contacted me. The question popped up in my mind to ask, "But didn't they tell you that you were chosen out of several thousands? There are only a little over 600,000 in Milwaukee and here sits a big percentage of those chosen? I don't think this is a coincidence!"

The others agreed that the odds were too high as well. For the first time I felt like I was at that meeting for some of the same reasons everyone was, to find some answers about the government connection.

I had initially joined the group because I had seen a couple of UFO's and had a general interest. I of course also had this inner feeling that somehow I was connected just a little deeper than it appeared. But as I have said, having self-doubt is a big issue when it comes to things of this extreme. So I like to explore things fully before I am convinced of something that is to be a part of me.

After hearing the others claims about these census people, the wheels in my head just started spinning, "They knew about my connection to UFO's before I did!"

I really had a hard time relating to everyone in the MASE group for awhile, only because I felt that whatever my connection was it was different from theirs. Some of the people in the group considered themselves to be abductees and were disturbed about most of the contacts they had. Then there I sat claiming to have only seen the two true objects I was sure of being UFO's, one being the saucer-shaped craft that answered my call in that lonely Iowa parking lot in 1990.

Then there was my first sighting I had of a UFO, which was no small event either though. It happend when I was with my friend Ronnie, in downtown Milwaukee coming down Fon du lac avenue which turned into the 4th and Broadway exit going east.

It was like February or March of 1990. Ronnie was driving when I spotted an odd, orangish-red, oblong object coming closer and closer to the car. I pointed it out to her and it was so large she thought it was the moon. When you looked up all you could see was this fully glowing object hanging there, without sound or distinct edges to the craft. But there was no missing time with this sighting because I kept an avid eye out for that happening, I knew how that worked.

But these two incidences were the main things I had to bring up in discussion at the MASE meetings. I also had one other incident when I was a child that really propelled me to look for answers not so readily available in today's society. This recalled memory actually happened prior to my coming across any material related to UFO's, and it was a shared recalled experience.

When I was about 5 years old, a sister of mine and I were met with a "mechanical clown" that came after us and caused us to both lose consciousness. We could never fully explain where that clown had come from and why we felt so terrified by it. Then after it happening we just forgot about it for 10 years as if it had never happened and then one day it popped back into memory.

I had a few strange events, but still I didn't feel that my strange happenings came anywhere near to the stories other people at the meetings were describing. I always did have a good time going to the meetings though. I found it easy to begin conversations with people in the group and we all tried to ponder our way through some of the mysteries presented.

The revelation about those census people was what really got me to realize that I had to find out more about my personal involvement. I almost didn't want to find out what it was. For the most part, none of these abduction experiences sounded like they were a treat. But I often found myself listening to stories from the other members and me saying, "Yeah, that happened to me, and that too, and…" Usually they were speaking about things that I would blame on a ghost or poltergeist. Things like seeing apparitions, objects moving, having dreams that you felt were tests, and stuff like that.

I now know that seeing ghosts and having poltergeist ̖ ̖
also related to the alien phenomena. It seems that if you are in tune ɯ
paranormal thing, you can most likely experience another. I have also
learned if you acknowledge one, other inter-dimensional things like, catch
word of it and spread the word around almost. But if I don't like what is
going on that is out of the ordinary, I try to ignore it and not pay it any
attention to make it go away. But at the time that I was first attending the
MASE meetings, I didn't know the true nature behind any of this stuff.

I was surprised by all of my admittance to experiencing so many odd
occurrences, but I still didn't feel "victimized." Many of the members did-
n't feel that way fully either, but for seem reason I still felt sorry for them
and some of their experiences. It almost seemed like some of them had
grown fond of their captors, as reported happening with people that are
wrongly imprisoned.

It's a survivalist act, that I'm sure conjures up when you feel you have
no means of escape but to make do with what you have. I also know of
some people that do not wish their abductions to end because it makes
them feel special, at least needed in some way. But I still didn't know for
sure where I fit in with all of this stuff.

But somehow the government knew to take the time to come and feel
me out to see what my views were on things. They even took the time out
to check out one of my sisters and did that census thing a couple of years
after my run with them. This is the same sister that had been present with
me during the "mechanical clown" incident and had seen some UFO's as
well, so I knew she had a connection somehow with aliens too.

Unfortunately though, she did not hear of my census ordeal. But when
she told me about some census lady coming around all the time to her house,
I told her what they were really about. She then immediately put an end to
her census trivia questions that she also concluded were a bit too personal.

But the census thing was not the last incident I had with some sort of
government force either. About two weeks after I joined the MASE group
I had an interesting visitor while I was mowing my lawn. I accidently

tripped over the extension cord to the mower, which unplugged it. Once the mower turned off, I expected to hear silence. But instead the sound of the mower was replaced by a big whomping, whooshing noise.

I looked around me to see the trees swishing back and forth madly. I then looked up and to my amazement, there it was! Just like in the UFO books I've read and television shows I've witnessed, a big, black, unmarked helicopter!

It was the same ones so many claimed to come around to shake the foundations of those who have witnessed UFO sightings. A brief moment of fright took over me, because I had never seen a helicopter fly so low and just hang there right over my house! But soon after my shock, I burst into laughter at how ridiculously obvious they were.

I mean the trees were flapping and the helicopter was leaning to one side as if they were trying to get a better photo of me or something. I was in the backyard at the time, but I looked around to see if my neighbors were seeing this too. No one was around and I wasn't about to give these guys a free show, so I did the first thing that came to mind and flipped them off and went into the house. I sat inside for about 20 minutes before they left, but then they would always come back.

I wouldn't even bother to poke my head through the window to see what they were up to since I could hear them just fine. Finally my roommate came home and the helicopter came back. I told her what was going on and I told her to look and see for herself. She was shocked and exclaimed that they looked like they were trying to land on the house.

I wish I could say that my brushes with obvious government forces ended there, but they didn't. They let me know that they were out to watch my every move, and learn whatever it was I knew. They pushed harder and deeper, and I held on tighter with white knuckles and all.

It was sometime in the winter of 1993 when they went the farthest they'd ever gone. I lived alone in my own apartment on Milwaukee's eastside, when I had one of those waking dreams. But this time something was highly different and not very dreamlike at all. In fact, I was wide awake in the middle of the night, in a place that was not my bedroom.

I was in a small office with large pane windows, and I knew that this place was located underground somewhere. There was vomit-green paint bordering the room with a pale yellow or off-white paint on the main part of the cement block walls that surrounded me. I was sitting in an armless chair, in front of a desk where a man in his mid-thirties stood. He wore a white shirt with a navy blue tie, and closely cut hair. He was leaning over the desk glaring at me, pounding his fist down and demanding at me, "You have to tell us where they are! You got to help us find them!"

I then remember straightening up in my chair, blinking a few times and glancing up at him in wonder. There was a guard standing directly to my right who was dressed in a typical, military camouflage uniform, holding a rifle.

"Help you? Find who?" It then began to sink in that something was truly wrong here and I exclaimed, "Hold on, where am I?"

Immediately following that statement one of them said, "Oh…she's waking up!" Then suddenly I was out again.

A twenty second "dream" in a military facility? I find it hard to believe that even in my wildest dreams that I could concoct such a story on my own. Unfortunately I would be met with another experience of this sort in due time, and it cleared up any doubts that these were real involvements of our government.

May of 1998, I found myself in the middle of the night standing in line in what appeared to be the same military facility as before. This time I was standing with my head lobbed forward, unable to control it properly, due to some type of debilitating state I was placed in. I somehow managed to maneuver my eyes ever so slightly so I was able to see in front and behind me to witness seeing others standing there in a line with me. All were in their pajamas as I was, but I appeared to be the only one with my eyes open.

Then as if on auto-pilot, I automatically shuffled forward when the line permitted me room to do so. I couldn't believe how my feet just moved on their own like that without my controlling them, and I admit it truly ticked me off that these same guys had done this to me again in taking me here. I stood fully awake in this pretty long line of folk in their jammies, for what seemed like an hour and half or more so my temper was just brewing.

I later found myself fully able to move about once I walked over this threshold and into this doorway of an old wooden floored gymnasium, common stock for an old military facility. Soon after passing over that threshold I was out of the gate, running and quite angry. I mean this whole while I was fully aware, thinking and waiting to get my chance to vent on my unsuspecting captors.

I remember being so enraged and thinking loudly in my head as I stood all that while in that line, "These freak'n @#!%* have brought me here again! They have got their nerve!"

Inside the gymnasium there were tables lined up end-to-end, along one side of the gym and people ahead of me were moving on down to the next table like clock-work. There were men behind each of these tables looking much like the one that questioned me before, wearing a white shirt and navy blue tie.

It now makes me think if an Air Force guy takes off his Navy blue, decorative jacket, you are left with the tie and shirt to match. So I'm guessing these were Air Force folks just doing some community service that no one knows about. It was obvious that they were divulging information from the people as they moved on down the line, herded like cattle.

From what I saw, everyone moved along pleasantly answering what was asked of them. But I guess I just wasn't having it, and let them have it instead.

I believe I headed to that first table and started off in saying something like, "What do you want this time? I'm trying to get some sleep for once and here you come again! I'm getting really sick of this game of yours! What, you want to know where the aliens are? Well, I'm not telling you." Perhaps some profanity may have come their way in the midst of it all too, I'm almost certain.

All I know is at this point in some way, I still wasn't completely aware of exactly where I was and that this was a real event going on. In my mind's eye, as I was literally shaking my finger at this navy blue tied fella and reading him the riot act, I felt pretty aware of all things around me. But it wasn't until an unsuspecting guy in a green camouflage uniform with rifle and all, came my way, before I found my true calling.

The pajama bottoms I happened to be wearing, were extremely large and baggy on me. So whenever I took a step, they slipped a bit at times. I didn't mind them since I only slept in them. But in taking a stroll through some military installment, the slipping took it's toll.

Well one of the camouflaged and armed guys that walked back in forth in the gymnasium, took note of these beloved pants slipping down on me. He probably thought he was doing a good deed in doing me a favor by reaching behind me with one hand and tugging my pants up for me. But while he was doing this I was busy telling the guy behind the table a thing or two when, "WHAP!" I whaled on this uniformed guy's arm for touching me!

It happened so quickly I surprised myself more so than the guy. I froze then, and just stared at the guy and said, "Oh my God! Not again! Where am I?"

I started to back into a corner of the gym, and several of the military guys closed in on me slowly as if to calm me saying I wouldn't recall anything, it was all a bad dream. Then "WHOMP," I was out again, or the end of the so-called dream.

I only recall these two incidences of being taken in the night by military folk. But it's really an unnerving thought knowing that even people are doing such atrocities to other people. The one connecting thought that I had about all this, is that apparently the military had a similar technology to the Shadows that I was able to awaken when either of them came near me. Almost like some silent alarm would go off in my head, and I would wake up with my captors unable to control me. Whether alien or human, I could always see the puzzlement and sometimes fear in their eyes that I was able to snap out of it like that.

Why fear? They say that humans are too afraid to lose control over themselves, why would another species be fearful that they did not have the control over you? Why would it be necessary, I'm pretty reasonable and am used to the presence of nonhuman beings and speaking to regular folk on irregular topics. So then speak to me as I am, that is if there is nothing to hide.

So many things, and so many unanswered puzzles.

"Who am I then to have military abductions invade my privacy like that?!" I was constantly bombarding myself with this question.

But it is also important to note I am not unique in these odd occurrences, I have heard of others recalling this questioning method too from military people. Myself and others must be onto something in order to have such direct measures taken on us. But then why not just kill us if they have us where they want us and we are not co-operating?

Think about it, what a great resource and backup plan to have if all else fails. If they are able to get at us in that manner and place us back in society without much knowledge of it happening, they can indeed continue to do it without much risk. But if you look a little deeper at those like myself that are not working quite on their side, you might be getting closer to the core of things and their reasonings.

They really know that we are not the bad guys here, and that in the end we'll be helping some of them out of their ruts they find themselves in. But then there is also the possibility they can't tell which of us is with which kinds of beings. If they are asking people like myself and abductees, "where the beings are," they are surely feeling they are being left out of the loop of some other beings and perhaps the ones they are in too deep with and now don't trust.

There's so much I don't fully have access to know about yet, but enough to make lots of sense. In living this wavering life of different realities it gets harder to decipher what is real and what isn't accepted to be real, and so we dismiss it. The lines are getting fuzzier and harder to divide what was once considered to be science fiction and true-life drama.

But then you get the thick-headed person that comes up to you and says, "Yeah, sure the government is trying to hide what they know about UFO's, and I'm Captain Kirk!"

It can really get to you sometimes, to take blows from people all the time that are afraid of anything outside of their little realities. For some people no matter what you say, even if the proof is there to back it up, they'll still deny these sorts of things away.

One friend of mine comes to mind that is a perfect example of this. Shelly is someone I have known for years and she knew about my interest in UFO's and we have spoken of it on several occasions.

Once she said, "I won't believe there's life on other planets until the government says there is!"

A couple years later, government scientist's did admit that they found life in rocks that fell from Mars, and Shelly heard this. I then asked her what she thought of life on other planets now and she replied, "Nope, I still don't believe it!"

She had also said she would believe it if she saw a UFO with her own eyes. Well, she got that chance too with one other friend of mine that was saying while they watched it, "Heidi was right!" You know she still didn't believe in the existence of life outside of this planet, she didn't even believe her own eyes.

Some choose to remain where they are in their understanding of things, because it is less work. Just to think on it a bit, all that we thought about how God made intelligent life, us, in his own image would have to be redefined. We would have to expand the history books in our schools to reeducate our kids on what other species there may be in the food chain. Our world defenses would have to be strengthened against the "threat" of a possible invasion. My God, if enough people would begin to believe in this UFO stuff, there would be a push for so many new bills, Washington would never be able to vacation.

To be honest though, I have really noticed a change in the numbers of people who are open to different possibilities now. People are beginning to realize how small it is of us to even suggest we are the only intelligent beings in this vast galaxy. Finally, what the governments have known for a long time and hoarded it, is now becoming realized through intuition amongst the people. Not to mention the new flux of television shows suddenly coming on the air, getting people to accept and/or welcome alien beings. Which could be a benefit to not be afraid of the good guys, but might let down our guards to welcome the bad guys unknowingly.

Why all this silence by the governments to begin with though? What could be so bad that they are afraid to tell us, we the people of forever loyal taxpayers who put food in their mouths? What has the government done that they are too ashamed to disclose to us?

I really don't think that our government's believe that, "The people just would not be able to handle the possibility of life out there!" Well, people who work for the government seem to be handling it just fine. But no, there's something more to their silence. They have done something that anyone of us knows better than to mess with. They have made a deal with the "devil" and they thought they could win.

14

THE PRICE WE PAY: *THE ULTIMATE PRICE TAG*

So many speak of how some of our technology has been taken off from downed UFO's. Some even say that some of our super advanced toys are expensive imitations from other races who have taught us how to do some cool meddling with our tools. Interesting speculations and according to Cafth and others, they are both true.

To get an idea how some of this technology trading may have taken place, I find it easier to look at examples from the past. So it's said, "you always learn from your mistakes." Let's see if our governments have really learned from their own mistakes in the past:

When the Native Americans or Indians met with the white man to trade items, interesting things took place. The white man gave the Indians guns and gun powder which made life easier for them to hunt their prey and fight wars with more success. As a fair trade, the Indians would give the white man items that were essential to their survival like foods and skins.

The Indians did indeed find that hunting became easier, where they could kill at a greater distance with the tools the white man gave them. Those tribes that became even closer to the white man, traded more frequently and therefore had more guns. These tribes were often more successful in battling and killing off their neighboring tribes thanks to their trading affair.

The white man benefited in surviving.

White men even traded or just gave out, nice warm blankets to the Indians, just to make life easier once again for the Indians. But of course these blankets were given only after having someone with small pox dance a jig in them and rolled about. Whole tribes were completely lost as a result of this act of malevolence and deception.

Early colonist had a goal in mind when they came to America, they wanted land. The Indians just happened to be here first so they got in the way. That problem had to be dealt with by any means necessary in order for the white man to have the land they desired.

Killing, enslaving and rounding up the Indians were some of the ways they were dealt with. Those that survived were kept on reservations in order to keep an eye on them and not just for baby sitting them either, as the United States government declared. The colonists believed that the Indians were incapable of taking care of themselves or handling themselves effectively. So the United States assumed the role of being the legal guardians of the Indians, where they overlooked their every move.

I repeat the facts of history in order to show that the old saying still holds true, "The more things change, the more they remain the same." Technology is often traded, with a heavy price tag. You may think that you are getting a steal by just giving up your simple means for someone else to survive. But in the back of your mind, one would have to think, "Geesch, this is too easy. I can't believe they would trade something so advanced just for some simple items!"

The trades that have gone on between human and nonhuman beings, is a topic of concern as well. Advanced technology and essentials for survival, are both highly valued. But which of the two can we do without? If you guessed technology, you would be correct.

If we do not **need** new technology, then why the trade?

It has been noted that we have a marked increase in our advancement in technology, so much so, that it appears that we have skipped a few hundred steps in it's evolution. So there is no question about whether or not non-local technology has been introduced to us.

Imagine, a race comes to you to offer their services to teach some of the things they know to advance you to a higher plateau. If that occurs, why, then you would be boss over your neighbors then right? No one would be able to come up against you in any war, because you had the inside scoop on how to make weapons that could literally blow your mind. As an individual, most would not find this amazing. But as a country, you would be all for it.

So you graciously accept the technology that these giving, friendly new beings have offered. But, what do they get in return? Oh, they just want to be friends and show how much they mean that. So just seeing us happy is satisfying enough. For some branches of our government, that is all they know about these beings. But there are others involved that know of the fine print at the bottom of their contract that has the total of how much they owe.

Just like those free blankets, someone or something made sure that our use of their gifts would bring grave consequences. The Shadows are those beings that offered to enlighten our government and guide us to our destiny. These Shadows have usually come in the form of the MIB's and various other forms to approach government heads.

In the book, *Men in Black Casebook* by Jim Keith, it is stated how MIB's have appeared throughout history at crucial moments in the United States. It is cited that during the signing of the Declaration of Independence and the designing of the U.S. flag, that a MIB mysteriously appeared to add his input then vanish.

They have always been around to guide and lead our country and others, on a road that they helped fashion. The United States is a great country to live in with a ton of freedoms and luxuries, I can't argue with that. But if you have cheated to get to that point, most would think that is not a good thing.

It is common knowledge amongst the decent aliens, that they are not to interfere with our progress. Even us humans have learned that we should respect the natural habitats of the creatures on this planet, if they are to survive that is.

Survival, that is the key word here. We are not wanted by the Shadows to survive, so they gave us the tools in order to kill ourselves and our easily and more quickly with. The Shadows want this planet for themselves, the land. They are looking out for themselves and are trying to have as much fun as they can in doing so.

I once asked Cafth why they didn't just go to an uninhabited planet for them to live. That way they wouldn't have to fight us and do all these petty little things to get rid of us. He said, that they would have nothing to do then, they chose to come here to do this to us. That they really enjoyed being a pain to us, just to see how far they can take it. Sounds like they are a lot like us, with that drive to conquer others and all.

Those of us that would survive an infiltration of the hybrids moving on in, will either have to render their support for their cause or give up their life. What's that idea that the Bible has in it, something about accepting the mark of the beast or be killed? Where the heck did these ideas come from, from so long ago? They had to have come from a similar resource in order for me to be sitting here getting the same round-about info from Cafth.

Parts of our government really have no clue about what they have gotten themselves and the rest of us into. But then there are those that are quite aware. But it all doesn't end with just technological treats, their involvement and use of their dark comrades goes even deeper.

Cafth began telling me about some of the details of our government's sneaky ways, "Your governments call on the Shadows for their ability to influence the citizens. They have taught them how to send influential messages through television, radio waves and directly."

When I heard about these tactics I really was not that surprised. I know that subliminal messages were used for simple things like in movie theaters to get people to buy popcorn and soda. Then I had heard that kind of practice was considered to be illegal and it was ceased. It probably has become government regulated so that only they can do it or something, I'm sure.

I always wondered about that subliminal stuff, because how in the world would we know if it was being done or not? Individually, we don't know enough to investigate what is being shoved in between the lines of what we hear or see. So really, what would stop anyone from using that kind of control technique?

Then it came into to my mind, "What are they actually putting into those subliminal messages?"

I asked Cafth the question too and he replied, "What are they not putting in them. You would be surprised what they are doing to make people comply with their views."

"Comply?" I thought. "How dare they try to influence anything I want to think about anything!"

Cafth would not go into much more details on it, because he felt he had given me enough info to understand the magnitude of what he was saying. He sometimes says, "You already know the answer." Well then, if I am following him right, this can mean a whole lot of things. Who knows, maybe we are made to support a new bill that is trying to pass in Congress. Perhaps, we really vote for political candidates that were previously selected to win!

If larger concepts like that can be thought up, maybe smaller and more individualized things can be conjured up too. Some people are all into conspiracy theories, so maybe there is a message that tells certain groups of people to get involved with drugs or kill one another. Dropping out of school, shoot up a school yard, or kill your parents, could also be on an endless list.

Some may wonder why anyone or the government would want to do such horrible things, and for what purpose. Let me tell it to you this way: When you are using someone else's old car that has a trick to getting it started where only they can do it, who knows what they are doing to get it going. The government is continually looking to the Shadows to work their technology to keep up the influencing going on for whatever purpose they want. So if the Shadows are *donating* their valuable time to help with this, they are free to do as they please for all our government knows.

What led me to believe that this sort of thing was going on, was when Cafth told me, "The Shadows lied about helping to control people, they are the ones who are actually in control."

I have told you how these Shadows operate, so they might do these kinds of awful things just to see if it can be done. It's all a big game to them and besides, it speeds up the process for them to take control even more so. Those people that have true spiritual inner strength and conviction about themselves, would not be effectively touched by their influence. But for those who are vunerable, need to watch out. Patterns are not formed out of mere coincidence, everything happens for a purpose.

Since Cafth left me to speculate on what he told me, I went ahead and speculated. I don't know how far all of this goes but I was reassured that it definitely goes deep. We are one of the most advanced countries of the world and also one of the youngest. Now how did that happen? Did we just get lucky in getting all the best minds from all over the world to move here? What are the odds of that happening, seems like another pattern to me.

The United States sticks it's nose and our young soldiers into everyone's business around the world if there's a UFO event or if we don't agree on what another country is doing. I suppose we are the number one protectors (and most obligated) of the Shadow's secret, so you will always hear of the U.S. military's involvement in things abroad. And a lot of the time we get involved in other country's conflicts for a good cause, but a lot is done for selfish reasons too. We are a country that values the freedom of the individual, and yet our country forcefully enlightens others to their ways. I don't get it.

I was told by Cafth that our government has been infiltrated by several nonhuman beings and they are well hidden by our policy of democracy. No one would suspect our country of trying to just go after selfish things. Who knows, they probably put a subliminal message on the air so no one would suspect them too. I am really just reaching here, but I am just trying to paint a scenario on the possibilities that may be going along with this.

I do know, via Cafth and partly my own recollections, that every time our governments call on the Shadows they and we are indebted more to them. Every time a person who either works for the government or not, listens to the Shadows, another is lost. If the government is providing the means for these Shadows to get their influencing across, they are betraying us all.

Whether some branches of the government know about the consequences or not, they still have to have a little common sense. As the laws of our government states, being ignorant of a law does not lessen our responsibility if we violate them. We are held responsible to be knowledgeable on things we are not fully aware of, so why shouldn't they also fall under the same jurisdiction?

Nothing is for free. We have nothing to offer these beings but our very souls, which is what makes them thrive. Having our souls is not essential to their survival nor is having a place to stay. Earth is the Shadow's home too now, they just want all that is living here to serve them and their goal. Getting us to do that, increases their numbers and ensures their victory.

As for our government reversing technology from UFO's that have crashed, that is going on as well. These various ships that the technology is being derived from, comes from both sides of this secret battle. Some of these ships crash due to the errors of those flying them and others have been shot down by our governments and other UFO's.

It is easy to see why the military would shoot some down if you understand that the government has been infiltrated. The Shadows use whatever means they have available to take down their enemy. The government knows there is a conflict going on, and like before, some know the reasons why and others don't. Some just know that they are invading our air space and so they attack or they shoot UFO's just for their technology. Then there are those higher up in command that are told by the Shadows that they are shooting at the true enemy. For the most part, few actually know what is really going on.

Sometimes when these ships are shot down, occupants survive and are captured and kept to study and interrogate. If it is possible, Cafth and his rescue their comrades. But they said they are limited in doing this because their technology is known, so they can be shot down more easily.

I realized that this was a horrible thing to happen, but I did not realize just how bad it was until I had a conversation with Cafth about the UFO crash in Roswell. It was the summer of 1997 and a group of people I knew were going to the 50th anniversary in Roswell, New Mexico, to celebrate the famous UFO crash that was confirmed by our government and then retracted in 1947.

When I told Cafth about what was going on in Roswell he said, in a very sorrowful manner, "What is there to celebrate?"

When I thought about that question, he was right. What was the celebration about? Most say it is a breakthrough, where the United States government first admitted that they had recovered a crashed flying saucer. But from an alien's perspective it would be a sick thing to celebrate the occurrence of an accident involving those they knew.

"We lost several of our friends in that crash and in several other accidents previous, and since then." Cafth added.

I could not understand what Cafth meant by losing them, especially since they had obvious ties with matters of the soul. So I thought it would be easy for him to connect back with his friends once they did pass over. But what Cafth had to say to my inquiries about his loss, truly threw me.

"My friends that were in that crash (Roswell) are trapped now on Earth. We were too late to retrieve their souls in their passing. The Shadows got to them before we could."

"The Shadows have your friends? How are they able to get at them if your friends work on the side of The Source?" I asked.

"It is a thing of war. We do not belong on Earth, but if we die there, we can be retrieved by the Shadows if help comes too late."

"Are they torturing your friends like the human souls that are there?"

"No. They cannot touch my friends. But they still sit there, trapped with misery all around them. They still suffer."

I felt horrible at the thought of these hidden warriors out there risking themselves to free human souls, only to find themselves trapped in a similar fashion. Whenever I personalize something like that, Cafth will remind me that I am not a part of the humans to be rescued either. That me and Amanda are also risking ourselves in this war to help out.

That made me think a lot about what was stopping the government or Shadows to come and kill me and Amanda. I knew about the Guardians and their role in protecting us, but I always look for more information.

Cafth answered, "You are capable of doing bad things too, such as killing. But something stops you from doing those things, another influence, The Source. There have been attempts on your lives, but they had a change in heart that was put there by The Source."

That made sense to me to think that God could and would influence people in the same manner the Shadows do. But what bothered me was knowing that there were other attack orders, other than Damian's, to come after me and Amanda! I would hate to think of what would happen if The Source wasn't keeping close, but I have faith it's nothing I need to worry too much about for the time being.

I really feel fortunate to know that there is someone out there, actually several, looking out for me. Everyone should feel good knowing that the same is true for them too. There are beings here that are only here because we need them. They are not looking for recognition, but they do not like to be grouped as having the same agenda as the ones most have heard of, the Grays and Reptilians.

Casualties of this war are mounting up and they are coming from both the human and alien sides. Cafth and his comrades are doing what they can to ensure man's true passage back to from whence they came. This battle is not just one to shake the Shadow's grip loose on our souls after we pass. No. These warriors are working in full force now because this planet is about to go into a phase. A phase where man will need all the guidance he can get.

15

A Place For Us: *Preparations Are Being Made*

When Cafth spoke of me and Amanda helping with the efforts to get people out of their ruts with these Shadows, it went pretty deep. All the people of today and past, that finds themselves either being pulled or tortured by these beings, do have the chance to be rid of them. Yes I did say past, as in those in spirit form, have the same opportunity too.

The plight to give them and all human souls that opportunity is the main part of the war efforts being fought here. The souls of people are being collected and unable to move on as they naturally do, and it's causing an imbalance that's felt throughout the universe. The vault doors of souls the Shadows have kept, are being knocked on and success is the only result that's being aimed for.

Cafth had mentioned before that reincarnation was something that humans did, that it was just a function of their souls. But once this mission and end result of this war is successful, there are going to be a lot of bodyless souls hanging around, I'd suspect.

I felt that this topic needed to be explored a little to see what would happen next to these newly-freed human souls. The Earth is already saturated with people, so I could not see how these souls were to return here any time soon. Cafth would later explain that returning to Earth was not the first goal they had in mind for the souls that are currently bodyless.

"We are preparing a suitable place for these human souls to reside." Cafth spoke up.

"Reside? Where?"

"Somewhere safe and compatible for humans."

"You mean that the souls will be able to take human form in this place?"

"No. Their souls will go there until the Earth recycles itself."

"What do you mean by that, how long is this going to be?"

"I have told you before that the Earth knows where it hurts and will heal those areas. This is a process the Earth goes through that will take about three years to be completed."

"Just three years? That's not so long."

"Not Earth years, it is another time frame that I cannot explain to you at this time. This process of the Earth will take much longer than just three of your Earth years."

"I see. But when this Earth healing process is going on, I have a feeling it is not going to be very tolerable."

"No."

"What areas are going to be the most affected?"

"Populated areas, like the cities."

"Should we move? Where should we go when this all happens?" I was of course concerned about this revelation since I do live in a big city, and it is only one and half hours from Chicago.

"You will know when the time is right. No area will be completely safe at some point. Eventually all human souls will be kept in the place we have prepared until things are corrected on Earth."

It seems that no matter what we do to avoid it, the human plight here on Earth will become futile after awhile. But at least there is a safe haven in the making for human souls to go to until the Earth is more suitable. I wondered what Earth would be like once all of the Earth's recycling was done. I could not even imagine things going back to natural means only.

"The Earth will be rid of the Shadows. Disease will be illuminated, humans will live as they were meant to. They will not die. I remember how Earth used to be in the beginning, it was beautiful and it will be again."

Cafth seemed to look forward to the coming times, although many hardships will be taken to get there. It made me wish for the new times to come too. I suppose after fighting such a long and harsh battle, it must be nice to see that an end is near.

When I think on all the deaths that are going to take place during the Earth's healing process, it makes me terribly sad. I look around everyday in my life and think how wonderful so many things are down here. That it is really a shame that things have to come to an end to bring in a new era.

I always have to be sure to be clear with my words, I really am anxious about things to come though too. I know that nothing will be lost, I have been told that everything and every species has been collected to be preserved. It is not the end, but a new beginning.

The Shadows are very close to being successful in their mission. They have a very large influence amongst many people, so human's are doomed anyways to suffer in some form. Dying once upon this Earth, only to suffer as if you died a thousand times at the Shadow's hands, sounds much worse. People may loose the vehicle in which they get around in today. But they will keep their very essences to "become" again someday, at least.

To be completely honest, I will not be one to weep the loss of my body. Of course everyone's concern is that they hope their passing is quick and painless, I can relate. But I remember what it is to be in my natural form and there really is no comparison that I can make to tell you how grand it is! I know that I am different from most since I am only one of a few that has survived of my kind from the original place I'd lived where the Shadows were victorious. But if human souls are at all similar, there is nothing to fear.

Imagine yourself as free-floating energy, with no strings attached. You feel, you see and you learn, in this state. But you must be ready and willing to accept your state when it comes.

Many souls will not be prepared or know what to expect when they pass and may run into problems that way. Most have heard of the explanation of ghosts and why they hang around. Some say they have either unfinished business or don't know or accept that they are dead.

If you do not know the signs that you are passed on, well then yes, you just might wander around doing your regular routines. Sadly enough, this actually happens to some individuals. Then there are some that are in this state out of pure cruelty, courtesy of the Shadows. But for those that are in this state due to their own lack of awareness, that is a good example of what I am talking about when I say some problems can occur while in transition.

Imagine, you're sitting home watching the game and at half-time you decide to run down to the corner store to quench your thirst with some alcoholic brew. You're in your car, you hit the gas when the light turns green. All that's on your mind is I have to get back before the game starts up again. You pull out, but some guy thinks he can beat the red light at his end in the crossing traffic, he hits you and you die.

You never really thought much about what would happen right after you died, but there you are. You're looking down at your body and you can't do anything about it. You think to yourself that you should have paid closer attention in church as a kid so then maybe you wouldn't be so freaked out. You start to panic, you look around and some robed beings show up. You think about the game you were watching and your friends and family you are leaving behind. You get a little angry that it's all over for you and these beings are trying to explain to you the rationale of your departure.

You listen, but you are still looking down at your body. Everything is peaceful and you feel the love of these entities before you, but you just can't handle this. You begin to refuse what is told to you, you never really were sure of there being anything after life anyhow. But suddenly it is all a reality. The beings want to help, but your denial is overwhelming and you begin to slip from their sight.

You slip down into a dark, deep sleep, until you are able to live and experience again. Until you are capable in remembering who you truly are, your soul's abilities and can let go of your brief life experience. You sleep until you can call out for help and guidance from The Source and other beings. Some even slip back to what they felt was more important, and are doomed to wander familiar earthly surroundings until they reach out for help also.

It is essential that you educate yourself at least about the possibilities of what may happen to you after your passing. You still possess freewill when your existence here ceases. If you are not one to learn now, you may not be so easy to teach later either. When we pass, doors don't just fly open for you to walk through. Everything is a process and the way through this process is learning.

I cannot stress enough about the importance of opening up now to different possibilities. You are being observed by others and The Source, but you are your own judge who lays down your own sentence. For those that still believe that God will judge us, in a sense you are correct since we all are a part of the whole and contribute to judge ourselves.

The sentences we will lay down for ourselves includes all the pain you have ever inflicted on an individual, animal or the environment. You will have the chance to feel that pain from the receivers point of view. What you do now decides what you are capable of later. Make yourself aware, at least. You don't have to make a faith out of it or anything either, just know, and it will lessen the shock later.

I tried to get the details on how this "suitable" place will be and I just ran into walls with Cafth. I did try to dance around the topic by asking if it resembles the Crystal City or Golden City that myself and others claim to have seen.

Cafth would not budge on this one, he just answered me back in saying, "I have good news for you. You will learn something very soon, so you can see for yourself."

Well, I have yet to find out what he meant, but I am content in waiting.

While Cafth was still on the subject of spiritual matters I thought it was appropriate to ask him about similar topics. Cafth will speak on the topic for some things, but when I entered into this next discussion, Soforus was offered up as a better advisor. Soforus then entered the conversation by coming right through the walls of Cafth's room to offer himself to my questions. I had always wondered about people who are comatose, where their spirits were while they laid in a coma, so I posed the question to Soforus.

"Are coma patients just sitting there in their bodies bored out of their minds or what are they doing?"

"No. They float above their body."

"So they can see and hear everything going on around them?"

"Yes, and if permission is granted, they may also roam the Earth freely."

That revelation was truly fascinating and comforting to hear. This permission granting thing was also a point that Cafth had made about some ghosts that roam too. Soforus did not explain what the permission granting is based on, but it was nice to know that our loved ones in this comatose state have freedoms too.

I used to think that when a person is brain dead, they were pretty much dead and passed on. But now I know that they really are around us, but sort of stuck in between worlds. I did ask if these souls were unhappy in this state and Soforus said that they were content. I am sure that they might be unhappy that their time is up, but at least they are not miserable and still get to observe their loved ones living their lives.

This state that these people's souls are in are kind of similar to the idea of astral projection. They are still very much alive, but they cannot animate their bodies anymore so they choose to pop out of their body to browse around. I touched on the idea earlier in this chapter, on how souls that are not prepared in their passing sometimes fall into a "sleep."

This state of sleep that can occur after someone's passing, is different from what a comatose patient experiences. Those in this spiritual sleep are stagnant, and not able to roam freely. Those souls are there to heal, become aware so that they may open up to learning and allowing guidance. No one is ever truly dead or lost. Everyone has a chance to exist and prosper as much as the next individual. Some people learn faster than others or some souls are older than the next, but we all still have a fair chance.

Opening your mind is of course the first step to making your transition and life go more smoothly. But you can make things even better by taking a few more steps into learning about who you are and your role as an offspring of The Source. We all, including the aliens, have come from the same Source. Therefore, we are all connected. So that famous saying that is quoted in the Bible from Jesus is true, "What you do unto your brother you do unto me."

If you strike out at anyone, you are only hurting yourself since we all make up a part of The Source. Everyone and everything is connected. No one can get away with hurting another and think it won't affect them in some fashion. Which is why the aliens cannot stand by idly, while humans suffer either.

They feel the pain being experienced down here. They cannot ignore the cries coming from those that once shared the same consciousness with them while in The Source. They are fighting to stop the tears and erase those that caused the pain.

A place is being prepared, and they will be waiting.

16

ALIENS IN OUR AFTERLIFE: *WHY THEY FOLLOW*

There has been a lot of talk about aliens seen when people are having a near death experience or an NDE. When I first heard of this, it was before I had ever spoken to Cafth and it truly frightened me. I really thought that the aliens were treading on ground that they had no business coming on.

I just couldn't understand how they managed to intercept our passing where they could actually meet with us. To me, that experience was one that was only to occur with God and His workers. Now when I think on it again, I find that I was not so far off since it has been made clear to me that some aliens do work with The Source or God.

When we pass or die, we enter another realm or dimension. We no longer need our husk of skin to get us around anymore. Instead we manage to move around by a different means, a force. This force is something that I would describe as being a kind of energy which is our true essence. It is the spark in our human form that keeps our hearts beating in our chests. I always found it funny the way scientists would try to explain the cycle that keeps our hearts pumping blood through our veins. They may have a reasonable explanation as to how the process works, but there is no way they can explain what started the cycle in the first place.

Without the human desire and essence being present in the body, there is no longer a need to keep the body going and so it wastes away, sometimes quickly sometimes slowly. Getting to that point of death happens in a variety of ways, and we know that they are not all very pleasant.

One time I heard of an interesting story of a man that was attacked and stabbed nearly to death. As he felt the knife passing in and out of him, he saw a light and heard a voice asking him if he was ready to go. He choose to stay here to take care of his family, but when the light was present he did not feel the pain his attacker was inflicting.

The most interesting aspect about this man's story is that he was left with a sense that he was never alone in his misery, that someone was always there with him and he would never die alone. This gentleman felt so strongly about this message that he now comforts families and friends of those that have lost loved ones to violent crimes. He lets people know that even in the midst of the most horrible deaths that can befall anyone, they are not left to suffer alone.

I was curious about what this man had to say, and wondered how this all worked out to occur in our passing. If what he had to say were all true, this would truly be a comforting aspect for all to know about. So I asked Cafth if he would enlighten me on the subject a little bit, and what he had to say about the topic was just what I was hoping to hear.

Cafth turned Amanda's head to one side, as if he were puzzled that it was not common knowledge and said, "What purpose would it serve to suffer to such extremes when the body is to die anyways? There is no sense to that, the soul is taken. Any movements that are made after the soul is gone are just reactions of the body on its own."

I am sure that initially the victim of a horrible death, does indeed feel the pain of what is happening to them. Those memories of pain are usually quickly forgotten though. Once the person has passed, they suddenly find themselves surrounded by a warm light that gives off overwhelming feelings of love and energy. It is no wonder that usually the trauma they have just endured slips from their minds once they are embraced in this manner. This is of course, not always the case as I have mentioned in earlier chapters. Several different scenarios can come about while someone is making their transition to their afterlife.

There is another important possibility that I think people should be aware of also. Aliens are capable of animating ones body while the soul or essence of an individual is taken elsewhere. Several abductees or contactees claim to know this to be true of their interactions with different alien beings. Cafth told me that they animate people so that it appears that the person is still present to ward off an intruder and/or keep up their bodily functions.

If the aliens are capable of animating us I am sure that this practice may also be done in a victim's final moments of life if they are suffering to the extremes. I am speculating on this as a possibility for why some of the actions of a suffering person seems to be as if they are present. I do not have the answer "matter-of-factly," but I do believe this to be a strong "maybe." I especially think this might be true since I have learned a lot about how those like Cafth and Soforus, cannot stand to watch an individual needlessly suffer.

Aliens are capable of interacting with our souls on a level where they can communicate and teach us things as they truly are. Astral contact with aliens is not an unknown and uncommon thing that happens, this is widely known amongst those that are familiar with UFO happenings. I have known about this myself for some time, and still it shocked me to know that people were having near death experiences with aliens.

This really should not be a shocking occurrence to anyone who knows about all the other astral contacts I have mentioned. If you have a relationship with these beings while you are alive, you will surely have one in your afterlife. Most people have heard that in these near death experiences, sometimes loved ones who have died are seen too. So why not see beings that you have known in this life also, that just so happen to be able to enter into your view while you are passing over?

I pondered thoughts like this to myself before I got the chance to speak with Cafth on the issue. Upon my adding the role that the Shadows play in our lives into what I was concluding about afterlife contact, I began to come up with more possibilities than I could categorize. I wanted to know how it was that mostly everyone that has had a near death experience, claims to see a light and then sometimes their loved ones. It really did not make sense to me that would happen, since Cafth had told me that 2 out of 3 people go to the Shadows. Did it just so happen that all these people were not loyal to the Shadows?

... responded in saying, "People in this near death state, see people and beings that are like themselves. If the people they are seeing were loyal to the Shadows, as they themselves are, that is who they see. If they were loyal to The Source, they will see people and beings they have known that also have the same loyalties."

It all goes back down to where your loyalties lie once again.

There are times where some individuals are given second chances when they are in this or similar state, where they are told that they can make a difference in themselves and clean their souls. This was something similar that Amanda had happen to her, just before she began communication with Cafth. No, she did not have a near death experience, but before she first started speaking with Cafth, she had a lot of private lessons taught to her. This is what she had to tell me in her own words:

"About a week before I ever spoke to Cafth, I was looking for some answers in myself. I just had a feeling that someone was out there listening that could help me, but I had no clue who, I just thought God was listening. During one of my praying sessions, that most people call meditation, I heard a voice."

"I don't know who the voice belonged to, but I knew it wasn't my own. It started to point out things about myself. I was shown my soul, and it had a whole bunch of black spots on it and I was told that I had gone too far away from them. That I had forgotten who I was, but I was going to have to feel the pain I had caused on everyone in order to come closer to my true self. They weren't kidding either!"

"I had to endure all that I had ever done that hurt someone, and I was shown what I did as I felt it. This was a long process and it took several days. After I went through the agony and pain, they showed me my soul again and it was clean. They gave me a fresh start and told me not to darken it again, and I'm going to do my best to keep it that way!"

"A fresh start," it does and can happen. I don't know what the circumstances are that gets someone chosen over another. For all I know, all those that experience a near death may have the opportunity to, but don't always regard it. I do know that in Amanda's case that she has a direct connection to the beings that work with The Source, so I don't have to wonder why her.

There is so much that I still don't understand about the different beings that contact or abduct people. I always hear that people say to the abducting beings, that they have no right to do what they are doing.

The general response of the abducting being is, "Yes we do, you agreed to this."

If people are agreeing to their abduction, or as in my case, contacts with beings, then they do have every right to communicate with us in any fashion we agreed to. I truly believe that if you did not want your contact to happen, it would not have. Yes you may be absolutely terrified about what is happening to you, but you have to find a way to annul whatever agreement it is that you made.

Perhaps some of the details were left out to fool you that you would come out ahead in this game, or you just simply forgot your loyalties. These Shadows come in assorted forms usually in dreams as whatever character they wish, whichever form lets your guard down to welcome them in.

Maybe you had a dream where they posed as your sister and she asked you to let her in your house and you did. You agreed on a different level, you know that and they do too. But you know something seemed strange in the dream, but you couldn't put your finger on it, but you still complied. Cafth told me that the beginnings of some ties start off in what seems, innocent manners. I ask, just learn to trust your instincts more if there is a next time.

Who knows how they managed to get you to agree individually, but they did, and most likely cheated in the process. I don't know. But I do know it is up to the individual on whether or not these beings are going to be a part of who they are for an eternity.

Eternity is a long time and if a person does not like the contact they are receiving now, then they must do what they can to end it. The Source is working at its end to help in releasing those under the hold of the Shadows, but it would help to at least meet The Source halfway. This battle has been going on for so long purely because it is the human specie's battle, where the finger can be pointed no where but in the mirror.

I know all the time I am constantly having to be on guard for attacks from Shadow workers in different forms. I still get met with peering eyes in the middle of the night, but thanks to some inner instinct, as soon as one of those guys comes near I'm wide awake. Then it's like this inner strength comes forward and shoots out of me, aiming to get rid of these dark invaders.

I just don't question that I can indeed get rid of them, having **no doubts** is the key. Once a hint of doubt slips in, you've created a crack for them to get at you. But to help me stand even stronger I say a prayer in the back of my mind the whole while, which helps a ton of course too. Often times even balls of light (the Guardians) come to my aid, pushing away whatever presence is near that's unwelcomed.

The intruding beings might plead with you that this is their right to have access to you and so on. But **know** in your heart, that is not the truth of the matter. Just flat out deny them, not out of anger, not out of fear, just out of **affirmation** and **faith** that you are not at their disposal.

Living this dual life and knowing of the few and far betweens, means never letting down and always having to be on the look out. It can get to be exhausting quite often, but not futile.

No one truly knows when all of this battling is going to end, and if they do know, no ones telling. So if an abductee passes away today or tomorrow, their enslavery just moves up a notch. Harsh words, I know. But this is what I was asked to inform and share on the reality of the situation and it's truly nothing new if you've ever heard of Bible scriptures. I'm still not so savvy on the whole religious bit myself, nor do I intend on going into any certain faith. But I remain very spiritually inclined and urged to encourage people to seek out on their own, more than anything.

God's put all you need stitched right into your DNA, everything else is there to figure out why things go the way they do in your body. It's obvious with all these religions and seekers in the world that it's engraved in us to look for something unseen, so it must be inside us somewhere. I wish I could go around and jostle some people a little bit to wake up though. I am only one person here, trying to speak out to many in hopes that the words I recall and have been told are heard.

When you pass on and you see different beings coming for you, you are just being led to finish the mission you agreed to. Only you know exactly what that mission is and where it leads to and if you don't, it would be in your best interest to find out.

No one likes to believe that they have ties with something not exactly positive, and it does not necessarily mean you are a rotten individual either. You could say that you somehow choose to hang out with the bad kids in school who were a bad influence on you, instead of paying attention to your parent, The Source. So whether you have those connections or not, it's good to know so you know if the path you have chosen is right for you.

Plus it will let you know what you are in for and whether you have been fooled to follow the wrong influences. But also keep in mind, that these beings like to continually heckle and test people that are on the right side of things too. They never give up checking to see if they can waiver you even the slightest. If they are really getting at you where they are leaving scars on you physically and mentally, then they are being successful to some extent and you need to get a tad bit stronger spiritually.

Tough times are ahead for us all, and we are all in for some surprises down the road. I don't think my puny little Earthling brain can handle all the information there is to know about this whole topic, but I do try to learn what I need. Educate yourself and prepare, if you can at least do that, I think things may work out for us all in the long run.

Fear shows ignorance. We only fear what we don't know. If we ask the right questions and boldly go seeking the answers, fear will seep away from our grasp, causing our eyes to open up.

17

INFLUENCES IN THE PAST: *MONUMENTAL MYSTERIES*

There are some who are still stuck on the supposed lack of evidence of there ever being any alien contact with humans in the past. However, it seems like alien interactions in the past stand to surround around some of the greatest mysteries on this planet. Some of those mysteries actually reveal some of the history of the Shadow's dark reign here. But these elusive places in question just get deemed to be a wonder of the world, at least they get some kind of title instead of efforts to debunk their existence as the new mysteries of today receive.

Some of these great wonders are topics I, of course, addressed to Cafth to help shed some light on. I'd hoped that these justified and officially acknowledged that some of the great mysteries on this planet might help bring some of the alien intervention into a broader prospective. And so that it may also show how long and deep the ties are that bind aliens to the residents of the Earth.

One great mystery that has baffled generations, are the great pyramids of Egypt. I always thought it was pretty convenient that the technology that was used to build them was somehow lost. It almost appeared as though people simply found it unimportant to pass down the story of how such great monuments were ever constructed.

I could see if these pyramids were a small feat. But for a people to wake up everyday in their shadow and not speak of it and move away only to rediscover them generations later. It just miffed me. How could they forget to pass on the knowledge? What I should be asking is, "Why would they cease to pass on the story?" There had to be a good reason why the secrets to the pyramids construction was not to be revealed.

Egypt was a powerful and highly advanced society in their time. They were on top of the world, they had all the riches and luxuries that they could have ever asked for. Reminds me a lot about the country I live in. That was not all that reminded me of the United States, I also wondered what price they had to pay to gain their prestige.

I had never really thought that way about Egypt until I spoke to Cafth on the subject. I used to think that the pyramids were so unique that they must be a very spiritual place. Many travelers to the pyramids also feel this is true, there have been many claims that their shape is one of energy and power. When I asked Cafth about the pyramids I asked pretty bluntly about it. I had heard so much about them and their *feel*, that I was eager to believe that there was some merit to the claims. I learned once again, that sometimes I need to look before I leap into someone else's beliefs.

"Did aliens help build the pyramids?" I asked emphatically.

"In a sense, yes." Cafth said quietly.

"Was it your kind that helped?"

Cafth did not make a motion that he was going to respond. I wanted to see if it was the good guys that helped make the pyramids, because then I would know for sure that the claims I have heard had some truth to them. So I asked another question that was a little bit more closer to what I had in mind to find out: "I mean, is it true that the pyramids have an empowering, spiritual energy to them?"

Cafth then made a disturbed look and responded, "Do you know what the reason was for in making the pyramids?"

"Well, I know that there are supposedly a lot of different meanings to various parts of the pyramids." I responded.

"No. I mean the real, ultimate meaning behind them."

I sat quietly waiting for Cafth to relieve my dumbfounded silence, then he said, "They were made to honor single individuals." Well I knew that, I thought he wanted me to answer the riddle of the Sphinx or something.

Cafth continued to say, "Anything that is made for the sake of self glory and selfishness is not a good thing. People were enslaved and died to make these monuments to their arrogant rulers. We would have nothing to do with making something like that."

Cafth told me this with the calmest demeanor you could ask for, but still I felt like no less than an ass for even insinuating that his kind had anything to do with the pyramids. What could I have been thinking? Of course I knew that the pyramids were built to honor pharaohs and wealthy men of Egypt. I don't know how I could have so easily forgotten what the basis was for these monuments, although many speculate and try to see them as possibly representing other things as well.

After putting myself down in my thoughts for a moment, I then realized that I was not alone in this disbelief. Millions had already flocked to Egypt to see the pyramids in all their glory and wonder. I do realize that they are a sight to behold once you bare witness to them. I would also be amazed to see such huge and mysterious creations too. But for the first time, I had truly realized that the pyramids were a place of horror and sacrifice. It seems that we have forgotten about the ancient cries that the people who built them must have screamed out.

I excused myself to Cafth for being such an airhead and posed another more reasonable question to him and asked, "Then if it was not your people that helped with the pyramids, I know there is only one other option. How did the Shadows help in building the pyramids then and why?"

"Influences. A human under the influence of the Shadows can be made to be very strong. The people lifted the stones on their backs, they suffered tremendously. Those that ordered the pyramids creation were also under the influence of the Shadows. Remember they can take different forms, even cats, whom Egyptians treasured."

I don't think it would have dawned on me that people moved these rocks on their bare backs. I knew that some sweat and blood had to be involved, but I thought maybe some higher form of technology made things a little easier. But in reminding myself about how these Shadows operate, it is no wonder why they let people suffer to create such a big empty grave marker. So many people read into every aspect of the pyramid chambers, overlooking the fact that a lot of horrible things happened to create these things.

I remember hearing about a mock experiment to recreate the pyramids using the same speculated process that was used by the ancient Egyptians. They used logs to roll the large cut rocks on, and the logs were crushed under the weight of the boulders. Minor construction was achieved, but they ultimately did fail to complete the project. How, who or when this experiment was done, my memory does not serve me well on. But someone thought they had it figured out and still could not pull it off.

One thing I do know to be true, is something I could relate to in what Cafth told me. It was when he said that a person under the Shadow's influence is very strong. Now I am sure most people have heard that a "madman" has the strength of several men. But that is not the only case where someone has extraordinary strength. When people become enraged and angered they can strike out with tremendous force. Then there are those cases where someone who is on drugs, also possess extra strength and lash out. All these case scenarios have one thing in common, the strength involved all came from something we associate as being negative.

I have said it before and I'll say it again, nothing is a coincidence. There is an apparent connection going on here with strength and negativity. It appears that when a person is engulfed with negativity they can do unhuman feats very much like the ancient Egyptian slaves, who probably did one of the most unhuman feats of all time. So then if the Shadows are the essence of negativity, they are responsible for the strength people gain. People that follow the Shadow's orders.

Thinking this all over to myself really got my mind in a knot. I knew there was evidence of instances when men have done incredible things that we consider not to be possible. But for men to pick up and move boulders that weighed several tons, that was just unimaginable to me. Then I remembered hearing stories about people who gained supernatural strength in times of dire need. Stories like the woman who lifted the car off from her child, or the man who kicked in a windshield to rescue someone from a burning car.

Just when I begin to loose faith that we are fighting a battle against a stronger opponent, I realize something. Love. Love has always prevailed as being more powerful than any force on Earth or any place else. When we reach into ourselves and get back to our roots of where we come from, nothing can stop us. The Source is a part of us, it is in us. There is no way that mere physical strength from an outside influence can add up to what exists inside of us all.

I had grasped the concept that Cafth was making about the creation of the pyramids, but the question still remained about the energy force associated with the pyramids.

Cafth went on to say, "The pyramid shape is an "energy magnet." They can be used to call spiritual beings to fulfill its purpose. In this case the pyramids were used to worship the Shadows, but they can be used to call on other spiritual beings, ones that are connected with The Source."

What he shared actually related to something that I recalled happening in my own past to me. While in my more true form and was being schooled on things to prepare to be born here, I was attracted to the pyramids and trapped in some sort of container. It was a horrible ordeal, but was freed by a person who was against the practice. It was a lonely and horrible ordeal that I faintly recall, but I learned my lesson upon being freed.

But what he spoke of also made it clear that the claims of people were partially true about them having an energy feel about them when near the pyramids. But for me personally, the history of these particular pyramids would send me looking for another source if I wanted to have purely positive energy coming my way.

Cafth had also indicated to me that the triangle shape is a symbol of a "strong point." That the triangle shows strength and conviction on all sides. Cafth said this is why a lot of those beings he works with have their names represented with a triangle in it, just as he does.

Since I had my questions answered on that topic, I wanted to move on to another topic of mystery, Stonehenge. When I brought it up to Cafth he instantly said, "(sigh) I knew you would bring this one up at some point." I think he was trying to be funny.

So I asked, "What can you tell me about Stonehenge then?"

Cafth began, "It is really sacred. It was a place where the physical and spiritual worlds were brought closer together. It was used for good and bad purposes."

I was not really sure what he meant by being brought closer together, so I asked if he meant it was like a porthole of some sort.

"Yes, you could call it that. It made people more aware of the spiritual world and it gave them hope about their spirituality and souls."

I was hoping I would not hear the same story about how the pyramids came about, but I had to ask, "So then could you tell me how this porthole was constructed then?"

"Guardians, and several different types of spiritual beings brought the stones from different parts of your world. But have you noticed that some of the stones appear to be missing?"

Another question for me, "Well, it doesn't look like it's complete."

"Some of the rocks were removed because they were not from Earth. When it lost its meaning, the circle was broken."

From what I could gather from Cafth, was that the purpose of Stonehenge was being abused. It was supposed to be a positive link between us and the other unknown worlds, but as always, it somehow got distorted. Cafth told me that it was the meaning behind the construction of Stonehenge that made it useful. So I suppose without the original meaning behind and supporting it, there was no use for it anymore. Sounded like a sad turn of events for something that sounded like a good thing to do at the time.

Attempts were made to keep a long enduring relationship between people and the spiritual watchers. I don't know whether or not it was man that did the screwing up on this project or the Shadows. I figure if it was men or Shadows that did, it is one in the same. I say that since men are not naturally trying to blow things for themselves, so they must have been under the Shadow's influence to have done such a thing.

The next evidence of mystery that shows there has been unearthly contact here, are the Nazca lines in Peru and land drawings abroad. These line drawings are done in very large scale etched in the ground, often traversing several hundred feet in the form of symbols, animals and people. It wasn't until men learned how to fly that they discovered all of the incredible and enormous drawings scattered around the globe. Funny how some of these drawings have gone unnoticed for so long because they can only be truly recognizable for what they are from the sky.

Some of these drawings, such as the 365-foot Uffington Horse in Swindon, England dates back to 100 B.C. If my memory serves me correctly, I don't think we knew how to fly back then. So how were these so called primitive folks able to create such large and accurate drawings? Being an artist myself, if I am working on a piece of paper 8 1/2" by 11" inches, I need to pull it back away from me to see that I have got things in the right perspective. Proportions and the flow of your creation is hard to get if you are not able to step back to see if you have things looking as it should.

So then the question remains, "How did these early people know that they were drawing something that was recognizable?" For me, this question was a lot easier to guess at than that pyramid and Stonehenge thing. But I wanted to get the full answers from Cafth, just to verify and make sure just how nonhumans were involved.

"The people were shown visions on how to make their creations. It really is not that difficult to make them, and they did make them on their own."

I didn't see how I would personally go about making anything like that, but I understand that men are very resourceful and creative. Digging out a design in the ground is one thing, but I still did not hear how they checked their work. So I asked Cafth to elaborate on the concept.

"As the people made these drawings they were continually shown visions as to how it looked from above. Sometimes beings took the people up in their crafts to show them how their work looked."

"Why exactly did the people make these drawings in the first place?" I still wanted to hear Cafth's explanation about the meaning behind some of these wondrous drawings.

"The people knew somebody in the sky could see them. They were used as a form of communication. Some of them were symbolic and others were welcoming signs for beings like us."

I had estimated too that some of these drawings were sort of telling about themselves and their surroundings. I really thought it was neat that the people, back whenever they made the different drawings, were more accepting about other worldly things. It seems that the more technology we got down here the bigger our heads got, to the point where we couldn't lift our heads anymore to see the sky for what it was. It's almost as if now we can't even lift our heads higher than our computer screens. If our computers can't analyze something or say it is possible to have happened, well it just didn't happen then.

There is so much around us that indicates that we, meaning Earthlings, have had some help. We cannot explain everything, some things just have to be left to faith. People are always trying to challenge on my proof of there being UFO's and aliens, as if I own the whole phenomena.

No one should even have to speak in that defense, they should already know what is going on in their own backyard. Proof is everywhere. If you see the need, give your neighbor's head a helping hand to help steady it in its gaze upward so that they may see the very wonders of the stars always above them. That is all the proof they should need to know that our star might not be the brightest one out there.

18

Supposed Evidence vs True Insight: What's Real

Most have heard of the claims of there being a "Man in the Moon." This is where you look at the assorted darkened surfaces of the moon with the naked eye, and you can kind of make out a face. You have to look carefully and some seem to see it better than others. I for one never really thought it looked like a face at all, but for what it was, deep caverns and valleys with overcasted shadows.

Now there is the new rage going on about the "Man in Mars." This one you cannot see with the naked eye, you need to have a high powered telescope or at least access to the nearest astronomy magazine to see this face. From the first photos taken, you can distinctly see what appears to be a face etched into the surface of Mar's rough terrain.

Several claim that this face is constructed similarly to the face of the Sphinx in Egypt. From what I have learned about Egypt, I hoped it had nothing to do with it. I think that connection to Egypt was encouraged by the fact that another structure was spotted near the face that resembled a pyramid.

For years people have demanded that this area on Mars be focused on and studied more, because some were sure this would prove there is life on other planets. In recent times new photos were actually taken, with supposed better equipment with a finer focus. These new photos would only show rubble and rocks in the place of the face that appeared in earlier photos.

Some in the scientific community feel that these new photos settled the claim, that the face was nothing but a poor photo of rubble. Then there are still others that say the new photos are fraudulent, that they were not taken at the magnification that they are said to have been taken. I don't know why the word of any government sanctioned or scientific community conclusion, is taken as straight truth anyway. So the question still remains as to whether or not the face is indeed a face on Mar's surface.

That was the question I then posed to Cafth. I really wanted to take advantage of the access I had to get some answers to some of these forever nagging questions. I must admit at times I really felt privileged over so many others that I could actually get straight answers in a matter of moments. While still, others have had to dedicate their lives in order to unveil the truth about matters.

But I never let my contact with Cafth be considered a casual relationship where I took him for granted though either. The possibility that his abrupt friendship may leave as quickly as it came, always stood in the back of my mind. So I made every moment in his presence count, with every topic.

"Is the face that appears in the Mars photos really a face Cafth?" I began.

"No it is not a face."

Cafth said this very matter of factly. But I could not understand this topic to be all that simple. After all, there has been a lot said on this topic and it really did appear to be a face. There had to be some merit to what it is we all see in this original photo of the Mars surface.

I pressed on, "What about the pyramids seen in the photos too?"

"Those are not pyramids." Cafth came to an abrupt stop once more.

I didn't know what to think about his responses, he was just too brief and pointed. So I pressed on even further, "So you're saying that these structures we see are nothing more than an illusion of the surface on Mars or something?"

Cafth took a deep breath and began, "When you see the clouds above your planet you can make several different shapes and forms out, correct?"

"Yes."

"This is nothing more than that. People wish to see more than for what it is. If you look hard enough at anything you can see what you want."

Well now it made sense why Cafth was so quick with his answers, there was nothing to what I was asking about. To him it was not even a matter to speculate on. I guess it was equivalent to asking about the Ferrari parked in my garage. Well, there isn't one. It would be pretty absurd for anyone to even ask, perhaps if I squinted and rubbed my eyes really hard I could see it. But that Ferrari is nonexistent, in my garage anyways. So I would give a flat out "no" answer too, and perhaps with an added tear. But it completely made sense to me now why Cafth took the stance he did. But still I had one other question to lay on Cafth before we left Mars.

"Was and is there life on Mars?" I just had to ask it!

"Yes there is life. But there has never been anything more than what there is now, bacteria and other small organisms that you cannot see with your eyes. But that planet is often used as a landing place to set down ships. It is kind of a resting area."

A "resting area?" Well okay, that was fine for me to absorb. But at least now that never ending question is finally put to rest, I suppose. It's like a part of me likes to still think there is a chance that at least something bigger than a germ used to live there. It's kind of a romantic idea that we weren't always alone in our little corner of this universe. That at one time we actually did have neighbors living under the same sun. Perhaps that is my human wishful thinking side.

Speaking of wishful thinking, something struck me about what Cafth said about that. How he said that people see whatever it is they wish to see. It made me think about all these sightings people are having seeing Mary or Jesus, from spotting them in a tree trunk to someone's bowl of soup. It has been getting to be quite a tremendous and more commonly reported happening, with people staking their claims on these sorts of sightings.

It was always in my mind that some of these claims had an ingredient of creativity. I have seen lots of photos and stories done on these appearances of holy figures and sometimes they really do look like the renderings of how artists depicted these people of the Bible. I have always wondered if anyone has taken into account on what denomination these people are that have these sightings too.

If a person is Catholic, I am sure they would see Mary in their soup, then say, Buddha. Then I am sure if someone were most any other denomination, you would see Jesus. It seemed that this phenomena catered to our ideals, as if to get a message across in some form.

I'm not knocking anyone's belief system in seeing these sorts of things either. I can't. Because I too have had one of the most tremendous experiences I have ever had when I got the chance to meet the man himself, Jesus that is. Previous to this happening in July of 1999, I knew that the man had existed and what He stood for. But He was someone that existed in the past, so I thought. Besides that, I had all I could to think on my new awareness of what my purposes were and I felt confident in my memories of who and what God was and my place regarding it.

But never would I think that I would have the opportunity to be in Jesus's presence as such. I relied on my own memories when it came to recalling The Source and seeing angelic-like beings with white robes and all. With all that I'd witnessed before, I figured if Jesus was around to be seen, I would have seen Him by now. So I assumed that people mistook angelic-like beings for Him because of the euphoria you feel when in the presence of these various beings, and just slapped the title of it most likely being Jesus.

I know that many think that Jesus and aliens are total opposites in terms of the spirit. Truthfully, before I met Him myself, I didn't know how to sort out in my head where He fit into all of this alien stuff either. I knew somehow He did since I knew God did, but it all escaped me on the whole schematics of it all. But I can say with one hundred percent certainty, that some beings work hand in hand with Jesus. Strong words, I know, and it's because of my encounter with Him that I can say that with no regrets.

I'm more used to speaking to others about the alien and UFO topic, but when Jesus made His entrance, He really altered my choice of topics there for a bit. I'd been asked by several people if His coming to me complicated or confused things for me more. But I'm happy to say, the only confusion came in when I thought on how I was now going to tell people about my seeing Him. Especially when people knew it was something I'd never dare to touch before in fear of sounding cult-ish or whacked out of my brain. But being who I am, I couldn't help but to be blatantly honest about seeing Him. And the calm my seeing Him brought to me about matters I still pondered from time-to-time, concerning where He fit in all of this odd stuff.

How I first met Him, Jesus came to me in a vision one afternoon when I laid down for a nap after work. It was as if I had just put my head on my pillow and sunk right through it to find myself standing in a familiar place and met with an approaching man. The scene was the front of my parent's home, and the man approaching me looked much like a friend of my sister named Robert, but I knew it wasn't him.

The man greeted me and I returned the favor, and then he asked me, "Do you know who I am?"

I couldn't believe my eyes in what I was seeing, and put my face in my hands in my general joking-like manner when I don't know how to respond and said, "Ye-e-s."

He then said, "If you knew who I was you would not hesitate to say it."

For some reason, perhaps because of the way His name gets abused and exaggerated whether in conversation or in churches, I could not say it. I instead said the Spanish version of His name and said, "Y-y-you're Jesus." But it's pronounced as HAY-soos.

He then said, "Yes I am."

Then He rose into the air and light seemed to emanate from all around Him, with a hint of what looked like wispy, white robes flowing from his body.

Then He began to speak and tell me all about His life and what His life meant, and what he accomplished. It was as if I listened to Him for hours speaking, fully aware of what was taking place. As He spoke, I even looked around and wondered why it seemed the floor was so close to me.

Then it hit me, "I'm on my knees, I don't even remember going on my knees!" I exclaimed in revelation to myself, then I looked back up in wonder to Him as he continued to speak.

After He finished I remained knelt there in awe and my mouth down to my knees as he paused and looked at me. Then I asked eagerly, yet nervously, "W-well, w-what do you want me to do?"

His first words were, "First, you need to show us something. You need to finish your book."

Of all things for Him to mention, not that I feel this book is ordained by Christ or anything. But it was very moving for me to be given such direct input that let me know I was on the right side of things. Then He went on into details that I should not be discouraged, that help is all around and to know that He would give me the words for what was needed to be shared. To remain strong in knowing that what I was doing was on the right path. He then continued speaking on about some other things that I cannot immediately recall.

But as He was finished and about to leave, I quickly remembered something that I had been wanting to ask. Cafth had told me that I was not to remember my real name, the one from my true origins, because I would recall too much about who and what I was. So for some reason I thought fast on my feet and as Jesus was beginning to vanish into the wall, I asked Him what my real name was.

I will never forget the true sincerity in His words and how they felt when they met my ears. Jesus laughed lightly and said, "I love you very much, Ileyah."

ILEYAH, what a beautiful name and what a wonderful gift He gave me in allowing me to learn that. I held onto those words, and thankfully Cafth's fears of my recalling too much did not happen. Nothing extra came to mind in my knowing this name, but I was forever content.

Soon after having this vision in this light dream state, I fully awoke and tried to move to go and tell Amanda about what had just happened. I was so overly excited about what just took place that I just wanted to go and blurt out this wonderful occurrence. But instead I found myself drifting back onto my pillow and into another in-between state that felt more drugged than anything, and was met immediately with another vision.

This time I was placed in what looked like a pitiful rendition of the scenery that I had in the previous vision. Something was not right in this vision and it became really apparent when something disguised as a family member of mine, approached me.

This person showed me the scene again in which I initially saw Jesus. Then they began to badger me for what seemed like continuous repeated attempts, to reconsider whether or not I had indeed seen Jesus or not that it was Robert all along who I initially thought it was. That my judgement could have been far off.

The fake person said, "Look again, there goes Robert now, are you sure of what you ssw?"

I replied, "Yes, I'm sure. That's not who I saw."

"Check again! There goes another Robert, and another one! Are you sure of what you saw?!"

I refused to give into their suggestion that I had mistaken Jesus for Robert. When this person saw I was not giving in, another "person" came running towards me in an attempt to kill me with what looked like an odd dagger. Then suddenly, I burst awake from this vision, shaken at what had just happened and I pounded on my wall to grab Amanda's attention to tell her what occurred.

Whatever had just taken place, I knew for certain that it was Jesus that had come by to encourage me. I also knew that the Shadows were not far behind in trying to get me to doubt myself and steer me away. They were so quick to try and steal the wonderful moment I had just had, that it really brought this battle up close and personal to me.

But it wasn't going to happen, I could have been blind and seen it was Jesus. Every cell in my body literally screamed His name, without being too cliche. It felt as if my DNA resonated to recognize Him, my help when it came. Just as it will be important for everyone to be able to do and trust when help arrives here to defeat the Shadows. I now fully understood that when people say they have had an NDE or vision where they saw Jesus, there is no way they are mistaken.

What should really stick in people's minds about this story is, it's not always wise to trust your eyes as to what presence is around you. Feel what it is, trust that your very heart and soul can recognize what stands before you. Visual imitations or likenesses can confuse situations, but it will become very important to decipher who's there to help and who isn't, in the very near future.

It'd also be wise to keep in mind, that this subject of Jesus and such is not so strange to be blended with this paranormal topic. Because the story of Him has been around so long, there's just this stigma as to how He should be perceived in such an ancient fashion. There's no question that the man did exist, that's just plain historical fact. But the belief that He was who He said He was, that's the part that just miffs people. It seems so much easier for people to acknowledge that a creator of some sort exists, but a part of that incarnate on this planet? That's just going too far for most. I guess it's because they don't feel worthy of having something they fear and revere as being so much bigger than they are, to actually visit here.

Before I had gotten over my inner fears of seeing aliens, I couldn't make out the figures I would see in my home. Not too clearly anyways. But once I let my mind open to the possibilities, I got to see behind the veil that I was catering and tending to, loyally.

There was nothing to obscure my view to make it easier for me to handle seeing something outside my immediate knowledge. I didn't have to look for anything or anyone to try and solve my personal mysteries, instead nature took over. My matters and other realities were naturally revealed to me once I walked away from my fears and assumptions of what things should be or look like.

Some would say that's "devil talk." That I let down my guard to the devil himself and that we should always have fear, the fear of God. I know of course it's good to have fear to some extent to protect ourselves and guide us at times, it's almost an essential emotion. But the voices of others do not cloud my judgement, but sayings like these are the words we have all been brought up with. It is these kinds of slogans that have ruled our lives and left us to gaze at our soup in hopes that we will get a sign of approval, yet still on our own terms.

Now we even gaze to our neighboring planet in hopes that they may be governed by a people under the same sun. It is a comforting and interesting hope to have, and I must admit I was a bit let down from Cafth's revelation about Mars too. I have really learned with Cafth on how to let go of some of my ideations about how things really are in this universe. This Mars thing was just another victim on my mental roster that I would have to check off as being too abstract.

Thinking abstractly is exactly what our governments are always doing. They keep trying to explore our universe deeper and deeper, sending out better lenses to get a clearer focus. But you really have to commend them for the efforts they have shown in seeking out answers about our universe though.

Or should we?

Cafth told me something pretty funny about the role him and his people play in some of the efforts our governments have attempted.

"Haven't you noticed how so many malfunctions occur with the equipment that is sent into space?" Cafth asked me this with a half smirk on Amanda's face.

"Well, yea. I've heard about a lot of mishaps about NASA's telescopes and various projects." I reacted.

"Well, you could say we have something to do with that. Sometimes we just make them…disappear."

I had to chuckle a little at this one. "You guys have been sabotaging some of their work? Oh, that's funny! But why are you doing this?"

I found it to be almost hysterical that aliens were making an issue to trash some of NASA's stuff. Especially because I know about the government's involvement with some aliens, and here they are trying to send out their little space junk, only to be drop-kicked by higher beings. To some this may seem only like presumed evidence of contact, but it cannot be a coincidence that billion dollar projects continually fail once in space after all the trials they run previous to launching them. The only thing not funny about the whole thing, is that it's the people's money that's getting trashed ultimately. So that means that the government will just have to try again and waste even more money.

But Cafth went on to explain some of their motives behind destroying some of these expensive NASA toys. He said that the United States and other countries, were trying to gain insight and access into a universe they are not ready to join yet. That humans have not evolved enough spiritually to work with and join a fleet like Cafth's.

I was told early on by Cafth that he was a part of a multi-specied missionary, where they would all join up to help out in a cause. One cause is of course the situation the Earth is in, but they also got together on other issues. A sort of United Nations thing, but really a United Planetary thing.

I thought it was really sad that humans had to be limited on their access due to a lacking within themselves. What it really is, is a lack of remembrance. People know that there is something missing in their life when they are born here, that's why we seek out different religions and faiths to see if it fills that empty void in us.

Above each individual there is a tunnel that connects us to The Source, that I mentioned earlier. These tunnels are often narrowed or clouded due to the negative influences that are welcomed on this planet and in our lives. But these tunnels once served as our direct contact to God, which is why when you hear of an NDE people describe going down a tunnel with a brilliant light at the end, The Source. The air needs to be cleared of this negative buildup so that the connection can be routed through again.

But I have to admit that I have seen, in recent years, that more people have been really getting in touch with more spiritual matters. There is even an actual awareness about the Earth's well-being. People are beginning to open up more about spiritual issues that don't only include Bible quotes, but are actually putting their own voices and feelings into words. There is a real awakening going on here, but it is still obviously a struggle.

But if the result of this struggle continues to show itself in the positive, I could not help but to wonder if we would be on our way to enlightenment as Cafth has mentioned is necessary. So I wanted to know, if at all, when humans would be allowed to join in on such an evolved group of spiritually in-touch beings in the universe.

He told me that, "The first step would be to eliminate the Shadow's presence. With them gone humans may be allowed to evolve more fully."

It always stems back to those elusive Shadows. It sounded like to me, that these Shadow's were trying with all their might to hold people back in every way. As if they could keep humans more under control if they did not spiritually evolve. For, with evolution comes awareness and if people are aware they might see whose hands are pulling their strings and holding them taut.

Of course then, why not put a hold on humans in opening up their extra eye, the third-eye (or spiritual tunnel). As some say, seeing with your third-eye is seeing the world around you from a different perspective. If I were a big green lizard who fed off from fear and ignorance, I surely wouldn't want them to see how I did it. Then they might find the way to stop me if they could actually see me in action.

"Yes, they have a hand in stopping the growth of humans." Cafth said in response after I questioned him about the Shadow's and Reptilian's role.

I was becoming less and less of a fan of these Shadow guys. It became really hard to continue to see and hear people speak highly about the Grays and Reptilians. All these claims about learning so much from the Grays or having great sex with the Reptilians. It was getting to be really sickening to be honest, but I could not blame people for being misled. It does happen to the best of us, and lines of innocence are being crossed anyways.

I got the impression in my mind that through this time of transition, when things here on Earth go through their changes, that will be the opportunity for humans to grow. This place that is being prepared for human souls will be a time and place to be given new direction. So many speak of a time of peace and tranquility that will come upon the Earth for a certain amount of time.

But you have to ask yourself, "Could this really happen with the same mind set that exists amongst people now?"

Of course that is illogical to even speculate on. If it were at all possible to have that kind of existence, wouldn't it already exist somewhere here, in even some small community? I would think so. But this is not the case. Something has to get through to people in order to show them the errors of their ways. Some think that God will just come and forgive them and they will be on their merry way to Heaven. It does not come that easy, and to even think that and fearing God at the same time, really makes no sense to me.

People have to take the time to receive structured lessons on how to express the true essence of their beginnings. How to get back to and associate themselves with the concepts that were initially meant for them to "be" in the first place. Man was not meant to be the power hungry force that they are today. These are not the qualities that are instilled in us, which brings me to my next piece of evidence that is not so well known.

As the saying goes, "There is good in all of us."

Every single one of us knows that this is true of everyone. Even if someone was a murderer, someone may still regard that person as being a good husband, son, or father. Love cannot escape us no matter what we have ever done in our lifetimes. How could that be there still, even though we sometimes do the darndest things?

That piece of goodness is in us because that is our foundation of what we were built on. These episodes of stupidity or rage is not essentially our own, but we must own up to the responsibility of expressing it. We do have the ability to suppress our urges or influences, and it is called self-control.

If our foundation is a positive one then our negativity must come from an outside source, which I am sure the Shadows would graciously accept credit for. Why not? It shows that they have accomplished something that remains to be a marker of our society.

...ave even heard stories that Adolph Hitler admitted that he took his orders from an unseen being that lived in the center of the Earth. I am sure that is why he sent scouts out to find an entrance to this inner world during World War II. Hitler was so terrified by these beings he would often collapse at meetings or wherever, while in their presence and appear to be talking with them aloud. Some like to categorize this as being schizophrenic, I like to think that these kinds of ill people just know and see too much.

This kind of evidence, of goodness being our true roots, is one that most of us can see within ourselves. I often hear people ask, "What is the purpose of this life?" This is especially asked when someone is down on their luck or experienced tragedy. Well I can tell you this, it was not meant to be this way.

Everyone is right when they say it doesn't make sense why some of the horrible things that happen in this life, do happen. It just wasn't meant to be, and it has been in the process where change is in the making of eliminating some things. This has not been an easy task, there is literally a Source over another Source here in the battle. The essence of one Source has to be removed in order to achieve change.

Battle lines have been drawn and parties from each Source are on guard. It's even evident that animals are making the choice, and that can be easily seen when you are bit by one dog and licked by another. Each side is so taut on their side of the rope to make sure they don't drop into the mud, but making the other fall victim to their actions. Where we will all stand when it comes down to it, depends on you.

19

THE EFFORTS: *WHAT'S BEING DONE*

Victory is the goal, but what are some of the efforts that are being made now on the part of the aliens and humans who are here?

During most of the time that I have been in contact with Cafth and Soforus, their team was usually focusing on an unspecified area in China. I would usually ask Cafth where he was located and what he was up to and one time he decided to let me and Amanda in on a major project of concern.

"There is a hole in China."

Again, a wistful response from Cafth that my brain could not interpret it's meaning fully. My mind then resorted back to my childhood, reminiscing about digging a hole in my back yard to get to China since it is on the opposite side of the world to us. Needless to say, I needed a little guidance as to what he meant by a "hole."

"A hole? What is it's purpose?"

"The Chinese government is digging this hole to gain access to the Shadows."

"Really? Don't they know what they are going to be met with?"

I was astonished to think that anyone would want to be met face to face with a force so powerful and negative.

"No. They think they can gain more power over other countries by having access to their world."

That really did not make too much sense to me, especially when there are some individuals in their government that know what these creatures are all about. I started to think about how the Chinese government is run, and realized that they were obviously influenced. But perhaps they wanted to show that they were powerful too by creating a front door access to the Shadow's world. This way, they may have thought, that they could have a little more control over what was being bestowed upon them by the Shadows.

I couldn't blame them for wanting access then, but still the fact remained that they let this influence in and were still trying to benefit more from it. They knew approximately where these beings resided, and they needed to gain more control over their situation. So why not dig your way to your solution? If you can't beat them, why not find a way to make more use of them?

My attention diverted back to Cafth and his concern over this Chinese project. Cafth knew what was being done, but I hadn't a clue what Cafth and his team were capable of doing to stop the Chinese activities.

"What are you trying to do about this project then, Cafth?"

"It is a difficult project and we have been working on it for a long time. We are in the process of making it less deep."

I wondered as to how he was going about doing this. If he was literally using lasers or something physical of the sort, I had no clue. Then I thought about how he and his people also used their power of influence to make accidents happen, for our own good of course. Just as the Shadows are able to place urgings to your psyche, the other side can impress things to lean towards kinder conclusions as well. Things may go against one's freewill, only in the case if something a person is doing was originally influenced by the Shadows. This method of influencing plays a major role in the efforts here to reduce the Shadow's control on Earth as a whole.

But, I knew if I would ask exactly what was being done in the case of this hole in China, Cafth might avoid the question or say that I already knew the answer. So I figured there were bigger fish to fry and that it was not that important as to how, only if they were successful or not.

"Yes, we have made progress. It is coming along okay."

That was good to hear, but it obviously was not an easy task since he always seemed to be over there working on it. I was already aware that there were other holes around the Earth that bore access to this underworld. But this was the first time that I had heard that there was an effort to make a manmade accessible entrance.

There are so many strange pet projects the world's governments are involved in. The United States is of course the strangest of them all. Billions and billions of taxpayers dollars are spent to send a few lucky souls to float in space to study rat poo and grow water crystals? I would rather it be spent on making sure no one goes hungry in our own nation so food pantries out of the generosity of churches and such, wouldn't be necessary. I don't recall getting a letter in the mail asking if it was okay to use my cash for some government vacation in space.

This is supposed to be the land of freedom and opportunity where the **people** run the government. It seems that somewhere along the line, the interpretation got mixed up somehow. But at least the government is taking the opportunity and executing **their** freedom to do what they please with our dollars and country.

Come on, what are they really doing up there in space and why? Why doesn't the American people question this more often too? I know that we have a lot of freedoms and luxuries that a lot of places do not, but I wonder if that is part of the distraction that causes us to entrust them with our future too much.

When the first man walked on the moon, we were all endowed to the glory of the United States space program. It is only natural to think that they would continue on in their space exploration. But I am really surprised that we haven't revisited the moon lately. Is there something there that they don't want to be too close to? Mars is used as a resting area and I know the moon is included on the map for that too, amongst many other things by some alien beings.

So instead NASA chooses to float their shuttles and space station projects in space. I would think having some kind of permanent footing would be easier to establish and perform scientific activities. Call me dumb, but don't we look at people that build along the California coast airheaded for not building on more firm soil? Then people moan and lollars go to aid those folk that were silly enough to sand that slid into the ocean. But here we listen to the ...... a floating space station and that's all we do, listen with no input. I think the word, "DUH" comes to mind very strongly for some reason right now.

If there is something on the moon or visiting it often, the question remains, why avoid contact with those beings that are out and about in space? As mentioned before, since the U.S. government is working with or are part of the Shadows, they see all other beings as a threat. But still there is more to this puzzle as to the reasonings behind their actions of avoidance.

Think on it, it's clear that the U.S. government picks up downed UFO craft here and there and takes them to places like Area 51. Area 51 is a secret military base the government denies existing, it's in the Nevada desert that is said to house several downed UFO's where they are studied and reverse-engineered in order to create and use some of the found technology. Many people have claimed to see odd objects that appear to be test flown barely above ground over the complex found in Area 51. Objects that some would equate to looking saucer shaped like the many UFO's reported.

If the government is able to get a UFO craft to rise up at all, one would have to think on this a bit. Don't you think that they would also take that baby for a ride into and beyond the great blue horizon? Surely they would be able to go to the moon and any other planet in a flash. That would be way too tempting to pass up for anyone. As one can imagine, this was another great topic for me to brush by Cafth with.

"Yes, your government has gone into space with some of these vehicles."

"And so, what happened? Did they go to other planets?"

"Yes, but we have not allowed them to return. They are not ready for that. This is an unnatural technological progress."

I grasped, from what Cafth said, that they indeed have done some joy riding in space. But once they ventured out of their Earth limits, those people were then committed to remaining away from home forever. I asked what was done with these people and Cafth said that they are living comfortably as possible on other planets or ships. Sounds interesting to me, but I would take it that these UFO pilots perhaps are not as thrilled.

I don't blame the alien beings for wanting to keep humans out of reach of something they have not deserved yet. These vehicles, in a sense, are like a stolen car. Casualties are often a part of the wrecked craft and our governments take them to keep as a trophy.

If I saw someone driving around in my stolen vehicle, I surely would do what I could to get it returned. But of course this issue is a lot deeper than just property. It is also about beings that have a non-interference policy and here they have an accident occur where their technology gets in the way and interferes with a natural growth process. Then there is also the concept that humans simply are not evolved enough to move up and out into the universe.

I then began to speculate to myself, "If the government already has this technology in their possession, who do they think they are fooling, with these shuttle-folk on board the Columbia and their camcorder recordings?"

It honestly seems then, that they are trying to keep the public entertained as they play with the real deal, higher UFO technology. I suppose in doing this they also keep kids dreaming that they may also do a space walk someday. But then when I look at it again, if the government had just suddenly abandoned all their space travel endeavors, a lot of eyebrows would be raised. They don't want any suspicion thrown their way, so it was best to keep up the front I would suppose.

Now then, this all makes sense to me. Then again, it also made sense why I had never heard of anyone report seeing a craft shoot straight up into space from places like Area 51. They aren't coming back! If they aren't coming back, it also made sense why the government is mainly just maneuvering these crafts closer to home and not abroad into space so much.

Then the thought crossed my mind that perhaps the government is realizing that they are more successful in space flight when they used their own technology. That they probably were met with less misfortune when they remained within their own means. Their exploration flights on UFO craft, I would imagine, probably did relate back a lot of information for them. But I am sure it did not equate to actually returning with materials and something to work with when they sent and used their own shuttle, equipment and technology.

So then maybe I was wrong about NASA being merely a front. Plus, then it would also make sense as to why they are putting so much money and effort into the space program. They know there is something to be had out there, but they are needing their own hands to reach it. I am sure some knowledge is still borrowed and that may play a part in the increasing number of so called "malfunctions" too.

But NASA is busily trying to do something. It is almost as if they are trying to find a way out of here. Now that thought rocked me a little bit.

Have they finally realized that the way this planet is going can no longer exist? I can't imagine that they are actually speculating about living on one of the planets in this solar system. These planets are totally uninhabitable for human life. I don't see that as being fun to have to create an artificial environment that people would always be restricted to if they did try to settle on a near planet. Humans need certain vitamins from the sun at a certain distance. I don't think our children would grow up very happy or strong in an artificial place like that.

If NASA was really speculating on living elsewhere, it would have to be another planet in another system far from here. It would also have to be a planet very similar to what makes up Earth. Humans are what they eat, and all the minerals and vitamins that we need to survive, exist on Earth.

So it would seem more likely that NASA and other governments are looking for a more suitable place to put up a fort of defense rather than a place to live. Since the Shadows are making it seem that the true enemy is out there in space and it is really their enemy not humans, I see why there is this effort. But there really are some beings out and about in space that are enemies of humans, but those beings work with the Shadows anyway. But still our governments wouldn't know that full story either.

Their true enemy is standing right behind them, waiting to stab them in the back without warning. Unknowingly and some knowingly, our governments are helping to build a stronger foundation to fight against The Source, of all things! It is just unbelievable to me that anyone would want to do such a thing like that. Looking to history again, the man who claimed to be the Son of God was killed at our hands and until this day there is a feeling of shame for that. But I suppose if you are under someone else's will, you would not be able to see the situation so clearly. Besides, all the promises of grandeur amongst the Shadows kingdom are probably more inviting anyways than a so-called "unseen" force who supposedly gave you this often painful existence.

It really is a vicious circle of wavering faith and insight in people's quest to dedicate themselves to the true meaning of their life. It is probably the greatest brain teaser that ever was. People do the oddest things in their quest for answers and guidance in this life. But there is no shame in that. Jump up and down if you would like, crawl on your knees for miles over rough terrain, do whatever it takes to rattle the cage you find yourself in. But if you do and still find yourself troubled, you have not sought out The Source to exist as it truly does.

The "powers that be" cannot be defined or confined to exist and cooperate as we would like them to. The Chinese government may think that they may gain an upper hand in knocking down the walls that separates them from the dark Source. Even if they are successful and gain access, that source would not appear nor work as they would like it to.

NASA is a prime example, they thought they could cheat a little to gain some insight on The Source, it's workers and the universe, through short-cuts in technology. But they found that they could not challenge that and get away with it. These forces are different, in that one governs us and the other offers assistance. But they are both similar in that if you try to cross them you will be put back in your place, one being a lot more gentler in doing this then the other of course.

It should be no mystery what side we should all be on in this war, but for some, their judgement is so clouded they cannot see beyond the back of their eyelids. Do not be misled. Our governments for the most part, do know what is going on. They truly believe that since they have been around for so long and so high up, that nothing can sink them. Sounds a lot like what was thought of a famous ship that sunk on it's maiden voyage.

20

WHAT YOU SHOULD DO: *SELF HELP*

In the midst of all this struggle between "good" and "evil" aliens, it could get to be confusing as to what to do with this newly transcribed information. I know when I was first told and recalled all of what was going on, I had no clue what I could personally do about it all. Especially since I felt that I didn't know how I was even to begin to relate any of this to anyone else!

I could just imagine blurting all this out on a street corner or something, trying to warn the world waving a sign or something. I would look like nothing more than some poor soul who lost their mind on some bad smokes. But when you get information as profound as this you really feel like running out and telling everyone about it. But I learned that was not what I was to do.

"Awareness," was the key word Cafth and the others instilled in me. I was to try to not make "believers" out of anyone. But to plant the "seed" and hope that it would grow in time for the coming transition.

I don't know exactly how things will come to change here on Earth step-by-step, but I was told about some tell-tale signs of some of the indications of the changes to come. One important sign relates to a certain vibrational change, like the very fabric of both the atmosphere and physicality of Earth. This change will begin in response to the various cataclysmic activities going on, such as volcanic activity, earthquakes, changes in wind pattern and so on. For many, it is realized that to some degree these sorts of occurrences are going on now on Earth.

Even human bodies teem with energy and at certain vibrational levels. The whole planet and its life forms are held together in a certain pattern

... in order to maintain their certain shapes much like droplets of water. Even color is based on vibrational wave patterns, with some having longer waves than others.

If these vibrational patterns are disturbed in any way, you could imagine the changes we may begin to see. Patterns will be expressed differently and solid things may then be held together in a new order. New colors will be expressed or exhibited in places otherwise not seen.

Other creatures rarely seen before will now start coming into view more frequently due to these pattern changes too. Creatures like those that have been termed as "rods" and "orbs" are some of these that will come more into our awareness. Rods are almost translucent, stick-like, flying, dragonfly-types with tails on it's sides like a dart. These are already starting to be caught on film all over the world, and will increase in regularity.

Orbs are often photographed and seen in areas of high paranormal activity and places deemed as having some sort of portals into other realms. They are generally, perfectly round, partially transparent white balls that float in the air. Upon looking closely at photos of these orbs, smaller dark spots can be seen on them that might make one think of these spots as their mouths.

When viewing orbs and rods, they seem to have some kind of intelligence to them due to their shapes and flight patterns. Some people speculate that these anamolies are some kind of undiscovered, perhaps even, trans-dimensional organism. Indeed they are newer for us to see them as often, but not new to existing or being amongst us. If other things are suddenly coming into view, perhaps other things may go out of view or change, even our own physicality may alter. How exactly we may change I'm unclear on, but it's something that I understand will come and pass.

There is also another type of creature that has come into view every so often, but it's so rare it's speculated as being almost mythical. These creatures are those that people report as being some kind of elusive lake monsters seen in various lakes world wide, the most popular being the Loch Ness Monster better known as Nessie. Nessie has been photographed in

Loch Ness, Scotland, appearing as some sort of a snake-like creature with humps on its back. I know of no better way to put what these lake monsters are about than putting Cafth's actual words in regards to them:

"The beast that is written of in your Bible in its last chapter, is in reference to these creatures that have been seen at times in your lakes. They will surface fully eventually, and take part in the Shadow's attempt to rule over the Earth."

These words of Cafth's have echoed in my mind for sometime now. I never did know how to categorize these various lake creatures. But to think that they were to be referred to as it was mentioned. I would never guess that his unveiling of what the changing vibes would bring, would relate to the *beast*.

But one other important aspect that will come along with these vibrational changes, is what other things we will be allowed to see. Our eyes will become more well in-tuned to what and who has been surrounding us for centuries, meaning the Shadows and other alien beings. The awareness of their presence will be markedly increased as we near closer to the time of the transition or changes of this planet and its inhabitants. This may be a horrible shock for some to bear witness to, and this is where some of this information I am giving is vital.

One must be aware and know how to handle the situation of what is occurring. For some, the transition will come so naturally that they will automatically know how to deal with the occurrences and move onto the "prepared place" with ease. Some, as I've mentioned before, may linger and become confused and even terrified and reject all that they see which does nothing to help their situation.

Just be **AWARE**, know that you can call out, know that there are others everywhere to help. Look to your Guardians and God for answers and help, now and always. Enable yourself to pull away from your ways of life as you knew it so that you may start anew.

These actions that you need to take are still a ways off, so we all still have to live in the here and now, but don't wait until the last minute either. The most important thing to do now while we are still in the middle of this astral battle, is be strong. Now you know that there really is a threat on your mortality and it is not worth your soul to say, get in the last punch in a fight.

I have really had to think hard on my role as an individual who was made to be a part of this Earth life experience to help out. I volunteered to come here in order to assist in awakening others to the crisis on this planet. But in doing so, I also had to become fully involved and accountable for my actions while here too.

I am also in as much danger to be lured by the Shadows as the next person. But because I am here to do a job or mission, I do have added protection which allows me to speak more freely on the topic than most. But the fact remains that I am still here for the long haul to endure whatever is thrown this way too.

We are all in the same boat on this bit of the adventure. If any of us are to get through this, we all have to pitch in to help one another, starting first by waking each other up to this reality. Cafth expressed that it is up to man on how we will destroy ourselves and I think that can have a lot of different meanings. Our physical demise is one thing, but to allow our spiritual knowledge to remain closeted is a whole other beast of its own.

I really don't push this sort of thing on anyone. This transition topic is nothing new to people, it is just not exactly like most suspect it to be. So if there is a conversation toying near the idea of the changing times ahead, I'll share. I just cannot always sit idly by and pretend to not know something when I do. In my lifetime I have only had to endure silence on this topic with some of the contents of this book, and it was killing me inside. But I was respecting the wishes of those that gave me and reminded me of the information to not speak on it at that time.

I don't really know what will become of my words once they have left my lips or my fingertips. All I hope is that at least one sentence of all my babble remains in the minds of those it reaches.

After all that I have witnessed and struggled to remember and understand through Cafth's and Soforus's words, I wanted to be able to walk away with a final conclusion in my mind about the whole world picture. But what I walked away with was even better than I could have imagined.

I got to know that our future is never quite set in stone as to when things may happen. But I know outcomes are usually just a matter of time before they come to pass. That revelation was kind of comforting and yet depressing at the same time. We have the ability to move time as we would like it to, but once our patterns are set into motion it is hard to break the flow.

I also got to realize that this planet is not essentially governed by Earth's true occupants. It is at the mercy of an infiltrating race that regulates the information that is passed onto the population. Information that is leaked only to slowly gain the acceptance and respect of their presence and superiority. Other parts are just leaked to give out misinformation that seem horrible enough to believe that is as bad as it gets (i.e. some aliens using humans as nutritional supplement) so we would stop at that and not look any further.

As a people of this planet we have to start to take on the responsibility to help rid Earth of this negative presence and horrible atrocities. People are having to rely on the aid of unknown friends, only because people blindly assist in making this planet home to the Shadows. This is a horrible bind this planet has itself in that we must all work to correct.

I almost felt ashamed for the whole planet when I thought about what Cafth and his people are doing to help Earth. I know that Amanda and I are included as part of Cafth's people, but we are also a part of this life experience now. I know people were not born to fend off unknown varmints, but there is such a thing called common sense.

"If you do bad things, you welcome in negativity." If you don't believe in aliens at least most have heard this message screaming out from the Bible or their own hearts at some point. This message is no lie, and it has been around for ages for a reason. That advice needs to be taken in sometime, this is not the time to ignore what has been said for so long.

In concluding my overview into what Cafth and the others wanted to be said in this book, I wanted to know what he thought would be the most important thing for people to remember in here. What he had to say really summed the one thing that we all need to keep in mind:

"Most importantly, it is essential for people to not forget their spirituality." Cafth stressed.

I could not have thought of anything better, because it is the one thing humans are truly lacking. We are always hurriedly running our errands, going to work and schooling our kids. Somewhere in the midst of all the hub-bub, we miss who we are. Most do not take the time out to seek out their true essence and get comfortable with it. Instead, most keep themselves busy so they don't have to think about things of that matter. Then comes this notion about fearing death.

Well of course you are going to fear death because you only know where you have been. But you have "been," you just don't recall. Thus, you do not know yourself.

For an "alien" to have to say "remember your spirituality" to us "humans," doesn't sound too alien to me. Not in the sense of how people depict the aliens to be anyway. They are in the same mind set as humans, but they just happen to know the true value of our souls than people seem to. If they are aware and we are not, we have a problem. Plus now you know that awareness is in the wrong hands, so most people are at a disadvantage on this planet.

These negative beings know no limits to themselves and look upon these 80% bags of water called humans, that can only see their limits. Guess who has the upper hand?

If you believe your hands are tied because these aliens seem all too powerful, well then your hands are tied. But if you can see that there is only a rotten being leaning over and whispering in your ear that your hands are tied, but your hands are really free, then you will be fine.

The message is this, "Take the time."

So many are hustling about making big deals about little concepts. They don't count in the end if you were a good cook or a hard worker or had a big house with a nice car in the garage. There's a reason why you can't take it with you when you die, if you could, you'd have a truck load of stuff to haul wherever you went. I wished these things got contemplated more often, but that only seems to take place when a loved one is lost and *then* you wonder where they went and why. It's nice to be someone or have stuff, but not necessary in the end.

I always tell people that all too often, *"People live their lives according to what they see, when they really should be closing their eyes to see what they live."*

Please take it to heart, and good luck.

AFTERWORD

If you would like to view detailed drawings of some of the various beings spoken of in this book including Cafth and Soforus, please visit www.UFO2U.com There is also a separate site for Cafth at www.CAFTHSPEAKS.UFO2U.com, where Cafth gives further insight. To help further research and the efforts to understanding alien contact on a more personal basis, please take the time to fill out our survey at www.QUESTIONS.UFO2U.com

To contact the author, please write to: heidi@ufo2u.com

BIBLIOGRAPHY

Keith, Jim. *Casebook on the Men In Black*. IllumiNet Press, Lilburn, GA, 1997.
Strieber, Whitley. *Communion*. Beechtree Wm. Morrow, New York 1987.

ABOUT THE AUTHOR

Heidi Hollis is the founder of the UFO and paranormal discussion group UFO2U and interactive website www.UFO2U.com. She has been looking into the UFO phenomena for over 15 years to address her own personal experiences and to help others speak more openly and frankly on the topic. Heidi also possesses a Bachelor of Science degree in Occupational Therapy with a minor in Art.

Heidi has a wide variety of activities she enjoys and involves herself in. She is an established comic strip artist, enjoys meddling in web design, has enjoyed CO-hosting paranormal talk radio, and writing articles for various formats. She is currently engaging in script and screen writing, where she enjoys bringing thoughts and ideas to life in production works.

Printed in the United States
4056